Mend the Mind
Mind the Body
Meet the Soul

Exploring the secrets
of health & longevity

Raj Kapoor, M.D.

LOST
COAST
FORT BRAGG
CALIFORNIA

Lost Coast Press
155 Cypress Street
Fort Bragg, CA 95437

Library of Congress Cataloging-in-Publication Data
Kapoor, Raj
    Mend the mind, mind the body, meet the soul : exploring the secrets of health & longevity / Raj Kapoor.
        p.   cm.
    Includes bibliographical references and index.
    ISBN 1-882897-27-7
    1. Mind and body.   2. Psychobiology.   I. Title.
BF161.K29   1998
613--dc21   98-28139
                                                        CIP

Cover design by Gopa Design & Illustration
Cover Image: *Shakti/Shiva* (gouache/pen and ink)
Copyright © 1994 by PennyLea Seferovich

Cover Photo: Elson~Alexandre

Book production: Cypress House

Printed in the United States of America

Dedicated

to the Supreme Absolute,

to the lineage of great yoga masters,

to all my teachers,

&

to all the writers

whose works I have read

To the beloved memory of

my parents, and

Jai Narain

&

Jiten

Acknowledgements

I would like to express my gratitude:

To Nirja, Sameer and Monica, for their unconditional love and understanding.

To my sister Manju for her encouragement.

To the friends who form the Sargam Music Group: Shirish & Bharati, Juginder & Sucheta,Ved & Alka, Hari & Neera, Subash & Suman, Brij & Usha, Praful & Bharati, for their inspiration and confidence in me as a writer from the very beginning.

To Peter Danes and Shantilal Shah, for their helpful suggestions.

To Lillian Konesky, for transcription, and Tish Doll, for secretarial support.

To Peggy Trevanion, for research and librarial assistance.

To Ginny Cole and Betsy Spearline, for their proofreading skills.

To Trinity Wise, for art and illustration.

To Cynthia Frank, John Fremont, and the staff at Cypress House for their support and expertise.

To the late Norman Hammond, for introducing me to my editor, Melissa Blum.

And especially to my editor Melissa A. Blum for it was her ingenuity and patience which gave life to these pages. Her editing brought clarity to my thinking and helped the manuscript evolve to its present form.

Notice

In order to ensure the privacy of the patients mentioned in this book, their names, circumstances and other identifying details have been altered.

Any applications of the techniques set forth in this book are at the reader's discretion. All matters regarding your health require medical supervision. If you have any preexisting medical conditions, you should consult your physician before adopting the suggestions and techniques in this book.

Contents

Revelation

It was a beautiful awakening.

One autumn evening, I had just emerged from my routine meditation to practice music. Outside, the leaves were drifting softly from the trees, a harvest moon was shining up above and a stillness seemed to blanket the crisp, fall air.

So relaxing was the gentle ambiance that the music soon ceased to be just an external presence of sound, and became an experience of *inner awareness*. There was an internal rhythm and vibration that seemed to connect me to the harmonies and melodies I was improvising. No longer were there two separate entities—musician and music—but a fusion of one.

It was as if the air around me had been heavy with a secret, and had finally shared it with me...like it never had before. Enraptured in the cosmic vibration, my entire being— mind, body and soul— participated in a dance of *awareness*.

Music is comprised of rhythm, melody and lyrics. The rhythm represents *time*; the melody, or notes, occupies the *space* between beats; the lyrics, like the principle of *causation*, reflect the mood of the entire composition. On that particular evening, the distinction between the rhythm, melody and lyrics was lost.

Immersed in the music, I found myself transported to a timeless, boundless reality. It was then that I could identify with the character of Monsieur Roquentin in French philosopher Jean-Paul Sartre's Nobel Prize-winning novel *Nausea* when he described music and existence... *"The turning record exists, the air struck by the voice which vibrates, exists...I who listen, I exist...Existence, liberated, detached, floods over me."*

Freed from the domain of earth-bound reality, my body felt weight-less, and my mind did not conceptualize the past or the future—only the "now" existed. The moment was short-lived, but so intoxicating and mesmerizing that I sought to recapture it. In all my years as a musician and yoga practitioner, I had never before experienced such *transcendence*.

I did not claim to have had a "religious experience," or to have been "touched" by a supernatural force, although any strange and un-expected phenomenon is usually attributed to such influences. Instead, I set out to explore the world of metaphysical truths or *timeless awareness,* and to uncover the answer to what the Tao-ists refer to as the "the Way."

My own revelation took me down the memory lane of the personal encounters I had had with the Himalayan yogis. I recalled their teachings of how deep meditation leads to *timeless awareness.* They defined this Universal Reality by the term *Sat-Chit-Ananda*—liter-ally *Existence-Consciousness-Bliss*—implying that it is eternal, self-aware and blissful. It has no beginning and no end and is always existing, because it is existence itself! Free from time, space or causation, this *awareness* is always inherently blissful.

In profound meditation, this mystical experience of reality was a momentous event for the yogis. It was a newborn awakening of human *awareness*...and an event that continues to shake the very foundations of our earthly existence.

Influenced by such an awakening—however transient—I felt self-inspired. I attempted to unravel the mysteries of the ancient time-honored secrets of yoga, and correlate these with the world-view of new age physics and modern medicine.

Revelation

The two foundations of twentieth century physics—*quantum theory* and *theory of relativity*—reflect the ancient philosophy of yoga. Exploring the atomic and sub-atomic world, I discovered that the modern-day theory is essentially an old one, returning us to a past that is thousands of years old. To my surprise, I found that yoga provides a consistent and beautiful framework that accommodates our most advanced theories of the physical world.

Not completely satisfied with the scientific information, my inner quest led me to further explore my revelation. Only by understanding the *nature of awareness* according to yoga philosophy, and interpreting its interaction with *human physiology* could I then convey my own "inner experience" to others and apply it to my patients.

As a physician, I understood that the predominant approach to illness in our time—modern medicine— fails to totally eliminate our sickness and suffering. It has shortcomings, maybe because it favors logic over wisdom and science over spirituality. And above all, I came to realize that a modern practice mostly treats the physical body as *matter*, failing to acknowledge the hidden force behind the matter: the *energy*.

Once this knowledge was revealed to me, I adopted a new way of treating my patients by applying yoga technique. The results were so effective that I became even more convinced about the power of inner healing. Working in tandem with contemporary medicine, I found that *holistic* methods like yoga therapy serve to enhance a modern practice...confirming that meditation *is* the best medication.

After sharing my newfound knowledge with several colleagues and friends, they encouraged me to publish my thoughts. I had spent several years exploring the holistic world, and after a lot of soul-searching, my research converged into the actual manuscript.

The idea was not to merely repeat what other scholars have said, but to offer independent insight explaining the intimate, unseen connection between the mind, body and soul.

After my own thought-provoking and comprehensive journey into the inner world, I now invite each and every reader to make the connection, or appointment, with his or her own *Self*. For those of us who would like to enjoy a more desirable, healthy lifestyle, this book is a must-read.

It combines the teachings of yoga and meditative philosophy with contemporary medicine for creating a state of optimum health and longevity. Providing scientific evidence for the benefits of a holistic approach, it is intended to introduce readers to my "break-through" concept of *awareness* and *aliveness*.

I explain how to enhance mental *awareness*, and how to control physical *aliveness* in a practical and comprehensible manner. I address the fact that as human beings, *we are energy* and *we need energy*, thus learning how to focus and direct this energy positively. Mend the Mind, Mind the Body, Meet the Soul serves as a novice's introduction, but is also a benefit for those with more experience.

It is really no wonder then that we are now witnessing a resurgence of the "new age" movement, as people are once again exploring the hidden secrets in the holistic approach to health and longevity.

Although yoga evokes many different images to many different people, it is not entirely mystical, or just another exercise fad. Above all, it is *not* a religion. (Although it should be practiced religiously!) Most of the world's religions—approximately two thousand years old— have incorporated yoga philosophy, which originated about five thousand years ago. Negating the mythical misconceptions about yoga, the book validates that it is a science and a philosophy.

Let the ageless, timeless wisdom of yoga be an offering to you as well. Let "the Way" guide you in enriching and prolonging your own life.

My awakening culminated in writing Mend the Mind, Mind the Body, Meet the Soul. Incorporating the ancient wisdom with my practice of medicine became the true purpose of my life. As a musician, physician and yoga practitioner, my calling became a gift to bestow on mankind.

Raj Kapoor, M.D.

Awareness is Freedom

All human suffering is ignorance.
Awareness is freedom.
-so said the Yoga Masters

At 28, Nicole suddenly found her life in full swing. Recently relocated in Pittsburgh, she accepted a teaching position for a class of 45 ninth-grade students. She was also engaged and planning a wedding, and the couple was buying and restoring a house. She had moved from her previous home in Maryland because her fiancé Bryan, a high-tech computer consultant, got a higher paying job.

Even though the changes in her life were positive and exciting, it was all happening too fast for Nicole.

She tried to recall how their hands had looked together when they tried on the gold bands for the first time, but the whole thing had been a blur. So had the last couple of months. While she had been constantly on the move, she had not been *aware* of what was going on around her. Instead of reveling in each new experience, she was just moving from moment to moment...and missing the larger picture.

She was so stressed out most of the time that her doctor gave her a prescription for Valium. When she was taking the medication, her symptoms seemed irrelevant. But when she forgot to take a pill, her doubts and anxieties resurfaced, keeping her awake at night.

One particularly hectic day, her after-school parent conferences ran late. Nicole and Bryan made it to their appointment with the jeweler to pick up their wedding bands with just enough time to board their flight to Annapolis, where they were closing on the house. Once on the plane, Nicole tried to relax. Without the Valium this time.

"I think I forgot how to breathe," she told Bryan.

It is probably safe to say that most human beings are like Nicole. Sometimes it seems that our lives are going on without us. We are busier than ever, with jobs (sometimes more than one), school, family, friends and many other obligations. We are always *going* and always *doing,* but are we *aware* of where we are going and what we are doing? Is it possible to become more aware of our lives as we live them?

During our waking hours, we are mostly limited to a certain physical state of consciousness. We are able to maintain basic survival, like getting enough food and water. In this state, we can also attain material goals, like go to work, raise children, pay taxes, play golf, see a movie and do the hundreds of other things that human beings can do. When we go the movies, we are sitting in a darkened theater and (hopefully) being entertained. For that fixed amount of time, we are able to suspend our reality, to enter into other worlds beyond our own.

To suspend reality within ourselves, to transcend the boundaries of normal consciousness and rise to a higher plane, requires more contemplative technique. It is this method of transcendence that is known as yoga. This process of returning the body, mind and soul to a purer, undiluted state allows you to encompass the "larger picture" that Nicole felt she was missing.

Nicole never realized that there was such a possibility before she picked up the latest issue of a popular health and fitness magazine she happened to find tucked into the plane's seat. Leafing through the pages, she came across a story that would change the way she thought forever. The patient in the article had gone to see a doctor about the chest pains he had been experiencing. This man smoked a pack a day, was physically unfit, and had a stressful job.

The doctor ran tests and made his diagnosis: coronary artery disease. He prescribed heart medication that would curb the palpitations and decrease the pains. But after a month of therapy, the man's condition did not quite improve. The pains had subsided a little, and his heartbeat was more regular, but the cardiac catheterization revealed that the arteries supplying his heart were continuing to harden.

No amount of the medicine would prevent the worsening of his heart condition if he did not make significant changes in his lifestyle. He was still smoking, did not exercise, worked long hours at a job he hated and had no hobby or other outlet to release his stress. The pills offered symptomatic relief but did not alter the underlying condition.

As Nicole read on, she thought about the Valium she was taking. Like the heart medication, it simply masked her symptoms. Popping the blue pills did not cure her stress. In fact, Valium gave her a kind of clouded reality. How was her situation any different from the unhealthy man in the story? His state of mind caused heart problems and hers insomnia, but medication was not the answer to their problems.

If modern medicine is the predominant approach to illness in our time, why then does it fail to totally eliminate our sickness and suffering? Technological advancements made in the medical field are entirely honorable. Doctors are able to provide a new lease on life by performing organ transplants, but the procedure alone does not come with a *quality* guarantee. Medicine alone is too superficial to influence all of the innumerable values that constitute a person's health.

A new, healthier heart replaces the heart that has deteriorated,

but what is to stop the transplanted organ from becoming cor-
roded if its owner continues to live an unhealthy life?

Because his condition was not improving, the man in the magazine article went to get a second opinion from another doctor. This
physician kept him on his heart medicine, but insisted that he quit
smoking, lose weight, and begin a supervised exercise program.
And meditate. At first, the man was skeptical. He would attend the
prescribed yoga sessions half-heartedly. Mocking the rest of the
"health nuts" in his class, he would laugh with his colleagues the
next day about the "voodoo" his doctor was teaching him.

But a funny thing happened. The more he meditated, the better he
felt. He was actually enjoying exercising, and had dropped thirty
pounds. He found it easier to concentrate and manage his time, so
his sixty-hour workweeks were reduced to forty. Most importantly,
he gave up smoking, and after a year of yoga therapy, he no longer
needed medication. A repeat catheterization indicated that his bur-
geoning heart disease had begun to regress.

When Nicole showed the article to Bryan, he scoffed and told her
that the man's recovery was a fluke. He was not convinced that
anything holistic in nature could usurp modern technology. Nevertheless, Nicole was inspired.

The body and mind have been so polarized by modern medicine
that most of us believe they are opposing entities. Doctors usually
heal the body and mind separately, and the mind is often considered a second-class citizen. What some do not realize is that our
physical symptoms are manifestations, or consequences of what is
happening in our mind. And the physical result—our ill health—is
making our minds even sicker.

Holistic is defined as *emphasizing the importance of the whole and
the interdependence of its parts.* Holistic medicine acknowledges
that in order for a whole human being to function properly, each of

its parts must be working correctly. If one part fails, the entire system is apt to eventually break down. The world is based on this natural law; how can our health be any different?

When we become unhealthy, we are violating the natural law. Ignorance of our selves—our bodies, minds and souls—is at the root of our ill health. If we smoke, our body will tell us that it is harmful by causing shortness of breath or chest pains. If we are anxious, insomnia or sleep disturbance serves as a reminder that there is something wrong.

Some physicians are recognizing this mind-body connection. Perhaps the key to achieving optimum health is maintaining a balance between the two. If the man in the article could basically cure his own heart problems by reaching such a level of coordination, why couldn't Nicole use the same methods to calm her anxieties, reduce her stress level and start enjoying her life without depending on a tranquilizing drug?

Yoga and meditative philosophy is ancient wisdom that has remained scattered for hundreds of years. For a long time, it had been confined to only those of Eastern thought or the select few who traveled to the East and sought to study it. With the resurgence of Eastern philosophy in the West, yoga is now available to anyone who is seeking a more desirable way of living.

It has now become so mainstream that many gyms and health clubs offer it as part of the curriculum. There are also personal yoga practitioners who instruct in the privacy of our own homes. More physicians are recognizing the benefits of meditating, and are passing the information along to their patients.

The patient Nicole was reading about in the article was introduced to yoga through his physician. She suddenly remembered the name of a doctor she had heard about in Pittsburgh. A year ago, while visiting her parents, one of her mother's good friends had become ill and had gone to see her doctor. When Nicole and her mother came to pick her up, she told them that this doctor was teaching her how to meditate.

The previously unhealthy man in the article became enlightened enough through yoga and meditative technique to prevent the progression of his heart disease. His quality of life had drastically improved. The friend of her mother's had embarked on her own meditative journey, and Nicole recalled how radiant she looked just this past year. Now Nicole was back in Pittsburgh, confronting the challenges in her life with only the tools of modern medicine to assist her. So far it was not sufficient.

The plane would be landing soon in Annapolis. She tapped Bryan on the shoulder, nudging him out of the latest issue of *PC Magazine* he had been engrossed in.

"I finally remembered the name of that doctor in Pittsburgh, the one who teaches yoga and meditation," she said to him. "I'm making us an appointment when we get back to Pittsburgh, first thing. What can it hurt?"

There are uncharted territories in the human body that we are not even aware of. Nicole felt instantly rejuvenated simply thinking about trying yoga; just imagine how she will feel when she incorporates it into her daily routine. Discovering the physical and mental within is her first step, as it was mine.

It is unfortunate that human beings are not born with a list of instructions like most appliances come equipped with. Some of us would never figure out how to hook up a home acoustic system or connect a modem without a manual. How do we then make the mind-body connection in the absence of a *health* maintenance manual? In the event of troubleshooting, is medical science the *only* answer?

This yoga synchrony between body, mind and spirit is responsible for optimum physical and mental health. And as we will learn later in the book, this same philosophy will enable you to attain the knowledge of metaphysical truths.

Bryan responded to Nicole's request that they pay me a visit with doubts.

"How can sitting on a mat and chanting help you de-stress?" he asked. "Medicine not based on logic or reason is just witchcraft, Nicole. If I can't see any scientific validity, then I just can't believe it works." Nevertheless, he agreed to go with Nicole, but as yet did not believe that each and every one of us can become more *aware* by meditating.

Nicole and Bryan would walk into my office as two very different individuals: she as an open-minded and hopeful recipient of the ancient wisdom, and he as the opposing and dogmatic skeptic of modern intelligence. Both would be making a beautiful discovery.

There is a legend passed down from the yoga masters, recalling the story of a rebellious young man sent to a monastery to learn the art of meditation. He would have to sit and meditate with the yogis, but resisted it. Taunting the masters who thought he had been concentrating, he would say, "I am sitting on the outside, but I am really standing on the inside." But eventually, the meditation was having an effect on the young man, and his whole attitude began to change. A yoga master passed by his room one night, and saw the man standing. Looking at the expression of serenity on his face, the master commented, "Now you are standing on the out-side, but sitting on the inside!"

I invite *you* to come inside, to join Nicole and Bryan as they set off on their quest, and to make an inner discovery of your own. Just take with you the idea that *awareness is freedom*. With that, the door to understanding has just opened.

Chapter One

Uncommon Wisdom

*As far as the laws of mathematics refer to
reality, they are not certain, and as far as
they are certain, they do not refer to reality.*
—Albert Einstein

On an early Wednesday evening in October, I meet Nicole and Bryan in my office, who just arrived back in town. Nicole had called me Monday, explaining her situation: how she finds it hard to concentrate or relax, how her stress is taking over her life. She tells me that the fading sun outside the window reminds her of the sun over the ocean, and how watching it set made her feel so peaceful.

"How can I learn to have that kind of peace in my life?" Nicole says.

The sun knows no darkness, though we as humans often see the dark side of things. I tell her that we nevertheless exist on the same level as the all-encompassing beauty of the sun. In yoga philosophy, everything from the finite minute particle to the infinite sky is interconnected.

"It sounds like mysticism to me," Bryan says. "Pretty, but not very scientific."

Since modern technology seems to have all the answers, Bryan wants to know how the teachings of ancient yoga could possibly enhance our lives. When we want to prove that a theory or practice is true and relevant, we look for scientific evidence indicating that it is. Only then is it given any kind of serious consideration or credence.

I have a very scientific frame of mind myself; it would have been impossible to become a certified physician without one. After years of medical experience, I still had questions.

In my quest to find the answers, I have discovered that the most fundamental one is *"what is the true nature of awareness?"* There are hundreds of books on medicine, and not one of them could give me a clue. The current methods of modern medicine are incomplete, and fail to address the real issue.

So I eventually changed my thinking, and let my journey take me back thousands of years, when wisdom was acquired without the aid of textbooks, scalpels or electricity. Physicians are only just discovering today what the ancient yogis knew, and that is the truth about our existence. After years of research, my investigations have led me to the conclusion that, interestingly enough, we have come full circle. The parallels between ancient philosophy and "new age" physics are so striking that I predict a revolution in the way doctors will see and treat their patients.

There are but a few physicians who acknowledge this information, because very few of them know about it in the first place. I refer to it as the "uncommon wisdom" because it is not widely distributed; in fact, it is mostly ignored since it seemingly does not fit modern medical standards.

I, however, feel an obligation to instill this wisdom to my patients and to anyone else who comes seeking answers, like Nicole and Bryan. Thoroughly convinced of what I have learned, I believe the knowledge can positively influence everyone's life.

There has been a recent attempt to correlate the two foundations of "new-age" physics— *quantum theory* and *theory of relativity*— with yoga philosophy so as to describe the sub-atomic world.

Nicole inquires how physics and yoga could possibly be related. Yoga celebrates *unity in diversity*, I tell her, and acknowledges that everything is grounded in one reality. We are indeed a *microcosm* (a part) inside a *macrocosm* (the whole), as yoga philosophers have long understood. Whatever is within us mirrors the entire universe and vice versa. When we truly understand and can relate to this concept, then we will be closer to the forces of creation.

Scientists themselves are re-examining the theories of creation and interactions of the sub-atomic particles in order to decipher the laws of nature. Their progress in high-energy physics has led to a *unified theory* of the fundamental forces, like electromagnetism and gravity. They have concluded, in fact, that a single *unified field*, is the basis of all diversity in nature. This discovery made by Western science echoes the teachings of Eastern wisdom.

By applying scientific theory and yoga philosophy, we have come to understand that human beings are networks of complex energy fields, and that energy makes up our physical cellular systems. We are born with the *potential* energy of *awareness*, and it is ever-evolving. However, the *dynamic* energy, or *aliveness* within us, must be constantly replenished from outside sources: air, water, food, and sunlight for sustenance. This energy is then restored during sleep. As for maintaining order in the system, both energy fields must integrate harmoniously and remain in balance.

In other words, *we are energy* and *we need energy*. The recognition that all matter is energy thus becomes the foundation for understanding how we are considered complex energy systems.

Through his famous equation $E=mc^2$, Albert Einstein proved to scientists that with *c* representing the speed of light, *E*nergy and *mat-*

ter are one and the same. He theorized that *Energy* was the true reality behind the matter, and that energy and matter are interconvertible because it is *all* a play of energy.

This directly opposes the earlier theory of Isaac Newton, who believed that the body was a mechanistic machine, an intricate clock made up of a very particular cellular structure. He suggested that our body was composed entirely of matter, and never accounted for the influence of energy in our physical systems.

Physical matter is nothing but an illusion of the senses. Both yoga philosophy and "new-age" physics describe matter as a substance composed of particles which are really nothing more than "frozen light."

"But if we dissect matter in labs and operate on physical bodies, how can there be anything less than the sub-atomic particles?" Bryan asks.

Trained to handle the complementary parts and pieces of computers, Bryan is much like Newton, and understands how *concrete* mechanisms work. Intangible, *abstract* entities like energy may seem difficult to comprehend, for they are the *unseen* forces behind the mechanisms themselves.

Conventional medical practice is based on the Newtonian model of reality as well. Doctors conceptualize the human body as a machine, or a computer, which is controlled by the nervous system. They believe that the psychological and physiological functioning of human beings is dependent on the physical structure of the brain and body.

Medical technicians have invented artificial replacements to substitute failing ones. Doctors do joint reconstruction, and have duplicated the kidneys' ability to filter through hemodialysis. Advancements in biotechnology supply doctors with spare parts to replace and aid diseased organs, but it fails to guide them on how to *reverse* and *prevent* disease and deterioration.

Modern-day surgeons are "bio-plumbers," removing the diseased component and re-connecting the system. Their study of biological clockwork mechanisms is sophisticated at the physical level only. Instead of using instruments, the doctors use drugs to target body tissues as another "quick-fix" for ailing bodies. Conventional medicine can not *cure* all illness by simply repairing or targeting abnormalities on the surface.

Doctors attempt to reroute hardened arteries like a plumber trying to fix a clogged drain. They use chemicals, a balloon plunger or even a laser beam to dissolve or remove the cholesterol deposits. More commonly, a new pipe is carefully implanted to by-pass the blocked artery. Physical "quick fix" solutions seldom work in the long run.

Cells *revolt* and *atrophy* when the realm of the energy field becomes distorted. To treat a recurring condition, this energy field must be addressed in order to redirect the cells. Most physicians, however, are hesitant about anything that can not be manipulated or dissected, like energy. This aspect of human physiology, or the domain of mind and spirit, thus remains largely ignored by contemporary medicine.

There is an unseen connection between the body and the subtle forces of spirit, and it is this relationship between matter and energy that the yogis found so enlightening. They understood this partnership, and utilized it to maintain optimal health.

Pharmacological and surgical approaches provide significant strides in the diagnosis and treatment of human illness, though their viewpoints only approximate reality. Human beings are more than a summation of chemicals and organs. What distinguishes us from non-living systems is that we are *greater than* our parts, *and* the sum of these parts.

Newton studied acceleration and gravity, and deduced various laws of motion based on nature. From these early experiments, scientists predicted how mechanical systems would behave. But Newton's models were unable to explain the behavior of electricity and magnetism, and could not account for the role of energy in living systems. New models of the universe were then developed to explain how the energy phenomenon relates to life.

Like the ancient yogis before them, scientists are uncovering the unseen forces of energy. They are looking to the body as both an instructional model and an energy field, and are discovering that human *awareness* is a field of energy. It is integrally related to the physical body, and participates in the creation of either health or illness.

Once the deep interconnectedness of the mind, body and soul is revealed to us, our understanding of the human body changes forever. A holistic approach to life can only serve to *enhance* a medical practice. Comprehending the concept of both *awareness* and *aliveness* will help doctors solve the mystery of why certain people seem immune to ill health, and why others are continuously subject to disease.

Bryan seems frustrated, but I am secretly pleased that he harbors doubts about what I have introduced so far. He is assimilating information like a thinker, not a follower. I assure him that new and different ideas challenge our perceptions of reality, shrinking some and expanding others. And though we are free to accept or reject what is exposed to us, our perspective of life is enhanced when we continue to learn.

The universal *macrocosm* and the human *microcosm* are both grounded in the same reality, and are thus interconnected. If it is the unseen reality of energy that governs us, what is the true nature of matter, then?

Chapter Two

Unseen Connection

Philosophy is the science
that considers truth.
—Aristotle

It has become common scientific knowledge that the smallest particle—the atom—can be further reduced to even smaller particles
called electrons, neutrons and protons. The yogis described the
parimanu, or atom, as the "smallest indivisible particle" which is
about 1/100,000,000 of a centimeter.

In order to visualize how diminutive this is; imagine an orange blown
up to the size of the earth. The atoms of this orange will then be as
big as cherries, a myriad of tightly packed cherries around the globe.
In a cherry-sized atom, the nucleus would be invisible to the naked
eye. To see it, we would have to blow the atom up to the size of the
biggest dome in the world: the dome of St. Peter's Cathedral in Rome.
In the now much-enlarged atom, the nucleus would still only be the
size of a grain of salt. And comparably, the entire atomic mass of a
70-kilogram human being would only be as big as the tip of a needle!

The concept of solid objects has definitely been shattered by atomic
physics—the science of the infinitely miniature.

All matter is composed of infinite arrangements of these minute
atomic and sub-atomic particles, like electrons. To a Newtonian
scientist, electrons appear to be tiny billiard balls, and have a predictable pattern of behavior. But further experiments have sug-

gested that the electrons *also* behave like waves of light.

Thomas Young's "double-slit" experiment demonstrated that a single electron appears to pass through two slits simultaneously, just like a light wave would pass several points of reference at the same time.

Nicole and Bryan were doubtful about the dual nature of these electron properties, and asked me to elaborate further.

In Young's experiment, scientists hypothesized that an electron may act like a particle *and* a wave, negating the fact that it can *only* behave in one way.

Yet, other tests showed that the same electrons *still* behaved like billiard balls: in one study, scientists aimed two beams of electrons at each other, and they bounced off of each other! Was it possible that electrons could display complementary behaviors of both waves *and* particles?

Demonstrating the very principle of complementarity, two mutually exclusive properties of energy and matter *do* co-exist within a single electron. An electron is neither pure particle nor pure wave, but encompasses elements of both. The basic building blocks of life—the sub-atomic particles—are thus twofold.

The wave-particle duality of the sub-atomic particles (like electrons) mirrors the relationship between energy and matter. This was elaborated by Einstein in the early 1900's with his $E=mc^2$ equation. Matter and energy are not the opposing forces they were perceived to be, but are *interconvertible*. Matter can be converted to energy and energy can become matter. At the point of conversion from energy to matter, the sub-atomic particles slow down, densify and give the *illusion of solidity*. Yet they still retain some wave-like characteristics.

Nicole confesses that this is hard to visualize, so I ask her to picture a fast-moving beam of light. Then I tell her to imagine that this beam of light has been slowed down enough so it solidifies and freezes, and is now a packet of "frozen light."

Our much larger, macroscopic *illusion of solidity*, or what we call the physical world, melts away when we delve into the sub-atomic world of particles. The atom is mostly empty space, and minute "frozen" sub-atomic particles fill the void. Matter is thus "frozen energy," not solid object.

The ancient equivalent of modern quantum physics— *vibrational densification*—is surprisingly validated today. Yoga explains the subtle energy fields that underlie and contribute to the functions of the human physical body. These are in dynamic equilibrium, and —like radio and TV waves—co-exist in the same space without interference. The subtle energy differs from the physical matter only in frequency, for matter is nothing but "frozen energy."

For example, through the influence of natural forces like heat and gravity, hydrogen and oxygen combine to form water vapor. The vapor eventually condenses into water, and with further cooling, this water becomes ice. The state in which hydrogen and oxygen are existing as separate elements corresponds with the *unmanifested* energy.

In the unmanifested state, there exists only *potential energy*, which has yet to form or manifest into anything. The energy from the two elements manifests in the form of vapor, water and ice.

In the process of human manifestation, the creation of the *first causal body* is analogous to water vapor. It envelops the source, or Spirit, the unmanifested, potential energy of *pure awareness*. The further condensation of the vapor molecules into water, and the freezing of the water molecules into ice represent the formation of the *subtle body*, or mind, and the *gross body*, or physical body. Water is denser than vapor; it is tangible, like the thoughts, and

9

perceptions in our mind are. Ice is more solid than water; the molecules are closer together, giving it the illusion of impenetrable solidity, as our bodies do. It is the energy fields that generate matter, and not the other way around; hence, the *body is an extension of mind.*

According to yoga philosophy, the complete human organism consists of *Purusha,* or pure Self. The Self is first encased in the *causal body,* then in the *subtle body,* which in turn is wrapped within the *gross body.* The Spirit or pure Self is the self-aware energy . . . *ever free, ever pure and ever wise.* The *causal body* is the "I-awareness" or the individual, the *subtle body* is the mind, and the *gross body* is of course our sensory-dependent physicality. (Fig. 1)

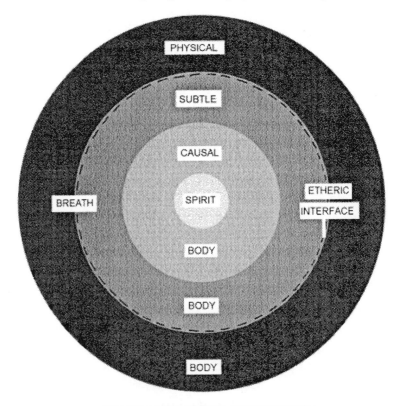

FIGURE 1. VIBRATIONAL DENSIFICATION

The Spirit or pure Self is known as the field of joy or bliss. This microcosmic field is the expression of both the blissful, dreamless deep sleep state, and the state of profound meditation. The empirical evidence for the mental intoxication that accompanies deep sleep and meditation are the body's production of natural opiates. The inherent urge in us to "get high" is thus a desire to return to this state of constant bliss, or achieving a "natural high."

Medical developments are slowly moving in the direction of these subtle energy domains, tapping into the multi-dimensional world like never before. Imagine the potential for physical diagnosis; right now, conventional methods do not detect disease early enough. But the growing trend of holistic medicine prompts physicians to recognize that for optimum health, human beings must enjoy the integration of mind, body and soul. In other words, healing must work *within* as well as *without*.

In contemporary physics, the universe is experienced as a dynamic, inseparable whole that always includes the observer, or the human element. This basic "oneness" of the universe is also central to the yoga experience.

The properties of any atomic object can only be understood through the interaction between the observed and the observer.

Bryan wants to know how *quantum theory* explains this. "Does this mean that we are the subject and the object, simultaneously?" he asks.

Max Planck's quantum theory states that energy occurs in "packets" called *quanta.* The quantum is the smallest amount of energy, and can not be sub-divided further. Sub-atomic particles of matter are very abstract entities—atoms can sometimes materialize as billiard ball-like particles and at other times, appear as electro-magnetic waves. Atoms, once seen as hard and indestructible little empires, consist of vast, unsettled territories of space. Quantum theory makes it clear that these particles are nothing like the solid fortresses that classical physicists once believed them to be.

In light, the quanta are referred to as photons, which always travel the speed of light and are mass-less. At the sub-atomic level, matter does not exist in a designated area. Like the flash of a photon, sub-atomic particles can not be pinpointed as to their exact destination; rather, there is a *tendency to exist*, a *probability to occur.* The laws of atomic physics are expressed in these terms of probability. No one can predict an atomic event with any certainty; we can only say that it is likely to happen.

As we penetrate the matter of the world, we find that sub-atomic particles are not probabilities of *objects* or *things*, but probabilities of *interconnections*. Nature does not give us "building blocks" to play with, but uncovers the intricately woven web of relations between various parts of the whole. In the web, we are interconnected as the observers.

The partition between "I" and "the world," and "observer" and "observed" is lost. Human beings who inhabit the earth are composed of the same reality as the sky above. Scientists who study their subjects also share the same energy as the subjects themselves.

The universe is experienced as a dynamic, inseparable whole, which always includes the observer. This is what the famous physicist Niels Bohr implied when he said: *"We are both spectators and actors in the great drama of existence."*

The revelations of quantum theory are inherent in the yoga experience, but modern science is predominately *experimental*. We want to know about the inside by looking on the outside. Try as we may to reenact life in a laboratory, we will never find all the answers if we go the external route. Instead, we must retreat within as well. If we learn to focus on the subtle level, we can make the "unseen connection" between the quantum reality and our inner world.

Quantum reality is in fact the blueprint of our inner intelligence. Like the dark, intergalactic space, the quantum field is an organized, silent continuum. Though the connections made at the quantum level are silent and invisible, they account for the "hidden physiology" in each and every one of us.

Thus, yoga is *experiential* in nature. The inner peace that comes from knowing true, silent reality can only be an individual experience.

In *Siddhartha*, the Nobel Prize-winning novel by Hermann Hesse, the young ascetic encounters the enlightened Gotama, and says, *"To nobody, O Illustrious One, can you communicate in words and in teachings what happened to you in the hour of your enlightenment... the secret of what the Illustrious One himself experienced."* Gotama Buddha can not reveal the secrets of reality or anything at all about his enlightenment. What the Buddha has experienced can not be expressed in words, or replicated in an experiment.

What the Buddha in the story experienced was *undifferentiated unity*. In such a unity, the traditional concepts of space, time and causation lose their distinction. Universal energy is timeless, boundless and ever existing. Like the Buddha, our *awareness* has the potential to be spaceless, timeless and without causation.

In a human *microcosm*, the static, or *potential* energy is *chit* or the *awareness*. It is an ever-renewing and ever-evolving energy system, and is never subject to disorder or entropy. In his work, Nobel Prize winner Ilya Prigogine defied the law of thermodynamics, stating that entropy is only valid if the machine is a closed-energy system. Applying this to the human bio-computer, or brain—an open energy system—he insisted that human *awareness* was *not* subject to entropy or decay.

In contrast, the dynamic energy—or the working force of the physical body—is called the *prana*, or the *aliveness*. *Prana* flows like

13

fluid energy through an intricate network of *nadis* or channels that connect the body to the mind and keeps the entire organism in working order. Unlike *awareness,* this energy is subject to entropy, and has to be constantly replenished. We need sunlight, food, water, and fresh air: we can not survive without the necessities before our bodies eventually decay and die.

From order to disorder, it is the *aliveness,* *not* the *awareness* that is subject to conditions and decay. Our *awareness* is indestructible, and a continuum. Such a "break-through" concept has yet to be understood and applied by conventional medicine.

Life itself is an evolutionary progression to higher and greater levels. By focusing our *awareness,* we can touch the pure potential inside all of us. A blissful state *can* be a part of our destiny, and optimum health is within our grasp.

The stage in which the meditation and the meditator—the seen and the seer—become one is *enstacy.* This concept is not to be confused with *ecstacy,* which is an over-powering, sensory-dependent state of mind. What the yogis call *Samadhi,* or *enstacy* is the most profound state of higher *awareness.* Seeking this reality, or meeting the soul, is the final goal of yoga, which opens the ultimate gate to human understanding.

Chapter Three

Seeking Reality

The eyes with which you see God are the
same eyes that the God sees you.
—Meister Eckhart

In the *Bhagavad Gita*, or the "Divine Song," the hero Arjuna has two desires: to experience the formless Brahman, or Universal Reality, in all its effulgence, and to see the formless and abstract Brahman manifest into concrete forms. For divine guidance, he turns to Lord Krishna, who becomes Arjuna's spiritual counselor.

Lord Krishna tells Arjuna, *"You are not able to see the whole of My form with your sense perception. Therefore I will give you a Divya Chakshu (divine eye) through which you can see the form of the Lord as a whole."* Only with a divine eye can Arjuna experience the entire universe.

I relate the story—this "Song of the Lord"— in the *Gita* to Nicole and Bryan, describing the fountain-head of ancient and intuitive wisdom. We as human beings can see several forms of the univer-sal reality, like the sun, stars and the moon. But our capacity to view the entire universe is limited, however. The naked eye will never see a cosmic hologram without a "laser mind."

How can a laser, a device that amplifies light waves and concen-trates them in an intense, penetrating beam, have anything to do with the human mind?

15

What science has discovered and validated through holograms and laser light, *can* be applied to what the yoga masters uncovered and reproduced through meditation and "laser mind." Bridging the gap between yoga wisdom and contemporary science unites the secrets of meditation with the modern-day magic of high technology.

At first glance, a hologram is hard to imagine without a concrete example. A good representative is the popular movie, *Star Wars*. In the movie, there is a beam of light that shoots out of the robot R2D2. The beam projects a miniature three-dimensional image of Princess Leia. The image is called a hologram—from the Greek *holos*, meaning "whole" and *gram*, or "message"—a three-dimensional picture made with the aid of laser light. The technological magic required to make such images is remarkable, enough so that modern scientists are beginning to believe that the universe itself is a kind of giant hologram.

Newtonian thinkers see the universe as a gigantic machine, and that the only way to understand it is to dismantle it, down to the very last sub-atomic particle. This mechanistic theory fails to explain the infinite interconnectedness beyond the sub-atomic level, which holographic theory can explain.

Holography, the study of pictures produced by laser light was first developed from Einstein's theory. The hologram, a three-dimensional picture created by energy interference patterns, may help science understand the energetic structure of the universe as well as the multi-dimensional nature of human beings.

The concentrated beams of laser light are so powerful that they are used in delicate eye surgery; no incision is ever made in the eye. Lasers can send beams of light from Earth to other planets and back again, supplying astronomists with knowledge of outer space.

Bryan believes that laser technology will enhance computer graphics, but is puzzled as to what a laser has to do with yoga.

The penetrating brilliance of laser light has the same intensity as a "laser mind," but to understand what accounts for such a splendor, we can compare the power of laser with ordinary light. If light from most sources tends to spread out as it travels, then the farther away you are from the light source, the less light you are going to see. Think of a flashlight in the dark. The amount of light it casts is not enough to see more than twenty feet or so ahead of you.

Regular white light, like the flashlight, is polychromatic; it is a multi-colored jumble of light waves, so the light emitted is chaotic. All the wave crests and troughs of the ordinary light are moving in different directions, like waves in the ocean do on a stormy day. The waves also travel in different phase relationships with one another. There is no correlation of time or space between the waves, making the light incoherent.

Laser light is quite the contrary. It is not dispersed and scattered, but a parallel beam, which spreads out very little. The collimated beam of the light is what ensures a minimal loss of power. That is why the laser beam can be a billion times brighter than the sunlight. A laser pulse fired at the moon produces a spot only half a mile wide after traveling a distance of 240,000 miles!

Laser light is also only one color, or monochromatic. All wavelengths but one are filtered out. The wave crests and troughs of the laser light coincide, and reinforce each other by moving in a perfect parallel line. The waves traveling in a definite phase relationship make laser light extremely coherent, as composed as a beautiful symphony. In contrast, the incoherence of ordinary light is like noise.

The hologram is produced when a single laser beam is split into two separate beams. Scientists photograph an object—an apple for example— using lasers. (Fig.2). The "working beam" is reflected from a mirror onto the object. The beam bounces off the object, illuminating it. There is also a beam being reflected forward. This

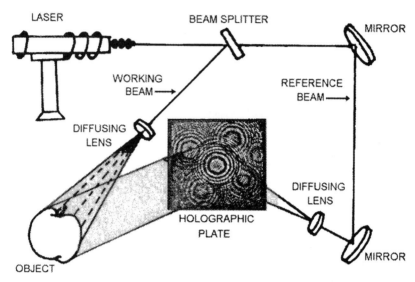

FIGURE 2. PRODUCTION OF HOLOGRAM

"reference beam" is allowed to collide with the reflected light of the first beam. This second beam penetrates the mirror, directing itself onto the holographic plate. Then the resulting interference pattern is recorded on film. It is this phenomenon of interference that makes holography possible. Interference is the criss-cross pattern which occurs when two or more waves, such as water waves, ripple through each other.

For example, if you drop a pebble into a pond, it will produce a series of circular waves that expand outward. If you drop two pebbles into the pond, they will produce two sets of waves that expand and pass through one another. The complex arrangement of ripples that result from such a collision is the actual interfer-ence pattern.

Any wavelike phenomena can create an interference pattern, in-cluding light waves. Laser light is especially conducive to forming interference patterns because it is such a pure, coherent light. In essence, it provides the perfect pond and the perfect pebble.

To the *naked* eye, the holographic image recorded on the film is a *meaningless swirl*, like the rings that form after a handful of pebbles are tossed into the pond.

Unlike an ordinary photograph that records only the wavelength and the light intensity, the holographic process records the *amplitude* and the *vibrations* of the light when it is reflected from the photographed object.

The three-dimensionality of an image *is* quite convincing, much like the one of the Princess shining right out of R2D2. We can walk around a holographic projection and view it from different angles as we would a "real" object. However, if we tried to touch the image, our hand would pass right through it, and like an apparition, there would be nothing there.

That's because the hologram is an *energy interference pattern*, an intangible, magnified image of the object, not the object itself. In such a pattern, *every piece contains the whole*. Unlike photographic film, each fragment of a hologram contains all the information of the whole. A millionth piece of the hologram would amazingly reveal its own miniature apple (Fig.3) when viewed through laser light.

So if Newton's theory was correct, splitting the whole apple into pieces would not reproduce other apples. Matter that is dismantled, including the apple, would stay that way. But modern science is beginning to prove that it does not remain fragmented. This is certainly a revolutionary way of looking at the universe.

Cosmic Lens

There is evidence that the entire universe is a tremendous energy interference pattern. And like the image of the holographic apple, every piece of the universe contains information about the entire cosmos. In such a universe, the higher levels of order and informa-

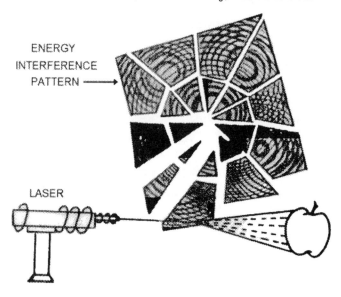

ENERGY
INTERFERENCE
PATTERN

LASER

FIGURE 3. EVERY PIECE CONTAINS THE WHOLE

tion are enfolded in the fabric of space and energy. Nobel Prize winning physicist David Bohm presented a convincing scientific argument for the presence of an "implicate order" of a holographic universe.

Unlike a static hologram, the cosmic hologram is dynamically changing from moment to moment. Overlapping energy interference patterns of multiple frequencies compose the universal hologram. What occurs in just a small fragment of the cosmic hologram affects the entire structure simultaneously. There is extraordinary relationship between all parts of the holographic universe. This holographic interconnectedness seems to define Universal Reality as omnipresent, omnipotent and omniscient.

Human *awareness* has the potential to view and decode information within holographic patterns on multiple levels by selective focusing. Evidence suggests that meditation leads to increased coherence of brain wave activity. A transition from incoherent random thought to focused coherent *awareness* as achieved in deep meditation has qualities analogous to a coherent laser beam.

The ancient yoga masters were thus able to view and decode a small piece of the cosmic hologram, and access the entire universe within the matrix. In meditation, they were able to focus their "laser mind" and unveil their discovery that... *the world is as you see it.*

Clairvoyance

Like the entire universe, the cellular structure of all living beings is holographic as well. Each and every cell in our body contains a copy of the master DNA blueprint with enough information to make an entire human body from scratch. Each cell comes complete with a master screenplay of "How to Build and Maintain a Human Being." DNA acts as a "director," informing each particular cell—the "actors"— about their part in the production.

The process of *differentiation* eliminates any kind of confusion between the cells. DNA would never instruct the kidney to perform the function of the lungs. This division of labor is responsible for the development of various tissues and organ systems in our body.

How do these newly differentiated cells know *where* and *how* to travel to their appropriate spatial locations in a developing fetus? DNA fails to explain this spatial organization of cells.

It is likely that a complex three-dimensional map organizes the cells. This field, known as the "etheric body," is a holographic template carrying the coded information necessary to turn the fetus into a human being. It also acts as a road map for cellular repair in the event of damage to the developing organism. While the DNA genetic code directs the cellular development, the "etheric body" unfolds the spatial orientation.

Geoffrey Hodson, a renowned English clairvoyant observed and lent some credence to the idea of an etheric predecessor to the physical body. The most unusual of Hodson's studies was his investigation of a developing human embryo from the point of conception to birth.

He recorded that the prenatal etheric mold appears very soon after conception. This etheric matter was a sketch plan of the entire human body. With his supernatural sense of "clear vision," Hodson saw the holographic energy fields inside the mother's womb settle into their appropriated places in the growing body. Given the limitations of ethics, modern science is unable to use invasive methods to study a fetus. Physicians do not want to take the chance of disrupting the pregnancy, so some have worked closely with clair-voyant investigators.

Like trillions of galaxies out there, there are 60,000,000,000,000 cells in the body. Not only does each cell contain the blueprint of the whole body; every single cell encompasses the "holographic" mind as well. Every cell contains the whole mind and receives signals. When we laugh, every cell in our body rejoices with us. When we are depressed or anxious, like Nicole, each and every cell is sad and worrying. It is no wonder then that our body is sometimes a breeding ground of *emotional toxicity*.

A new field of Psycho-neuro-immunology has emerged in modern medicine, confirming this. Studies show that the loss of a spouse causes such severe depression that the effective immune cell population is dangerously reduced during the bereavement period. Significant illness is not uncommon in such individuals, and often, the widow or widower dies within several months of the death of their spouse.

Like a change from ordinary light to the brilliant power of a laser beam, a transition from random thoughts to focused *awareness* in meditation leads to a "laser mind."

Laser light can penetrate steel, but the meditative "laser mind" can purge the emotional overload and decode the cosmic hologram, climbing the path that leads to a higher reality.

Seeking reality from the Lord, Arjuna is granted the yogic vision. The Lord says to him, *"See My multifarious, divine forms of many hues and configurations, by hundreds and by thousands....Today see the entire world with everything animate and inanimate, here dwelling in one..."*

Lord Krishna has enabled Arjuna to see with his own "divine eye" ...creating for him a laser state of mind.

Chapter Four

Beyond the Mind

There is something beyond our mind
which abides in silence within our mind.
It is the supreme mystery beyond thought.
Let one's mind rest upon that.
—Maitri Upanishad

If the coherent light of a laser can actually burn a hole through a steel plate, just think of what the coherent mind of the meditator can explore!

The average human thought is as random and incoherent as the light from an ordinary source. As we found out in the chapter before, laser light is highly focused and collimated, and our coherent *awareness* is the same when we meditate.

Without concentration, you can not learn or retain much information. Your mind is not synchronized because your energy is unfocused. The yogis learned to control their energy by meditation; without it, they found that the human mind tends to run a little haywire without such focus. It is an effect they called "scatter-brain."

Nicole confides that she often loses things, forgets appointments and sometimes, can not focus at all. She tells me that all the "have-to-dos" and "must-dos" clouding her head are making her thinking fuzzy.

24

When our minds are unnecessarily cluttered, they function like ordinary light bulbs: the light is diffused. However, with a "laser mind," our thought process becomes bright and penetrating. Those who meditate are able to cleanse their minds of non-essential thoughts. Their minds are like the single powerful beam of laser, able to fathom the fringes of infinity.

Scientists can not decode a hologram without using a laser light and yogis can not reach an enlightened state without using a "laser mind." Focus *awareness* as the laser focuses its light, and the cranium becomes a laserium, so that the mind comes to understand true reality.

Meditative concentration is so powerful that we can penetrate the unconscious—presumably an area of the mind only probed during deep dreamless sleep. When we meditate, we are so focused that our mind purges the mundane to make room for the magical.

The inner balance that Nicole is seeking in her life is not as inaccessible as it is believed to be. We all have the ability to filter out incoming stimuli from the outside world, and minimize the crosscurrents of the conscious and the unconscious mind.

A balanced mind reduces the stress on our body. Nicole reacts so much to the outside environment that her body is unable to utilize energy effectively, or relax. She is so anxious that she takes Valium regularly, so achieving natural peace alludes her. What she will eventually get from yoga is not a tranquilizing drug, but *tranquility*—a stronger concentration, a greater coordination between mind and body. Valium only serves to weaken her reserves further, enabling her to become dependent on a drug to cope with everyday life.

The deepest state of physiological balance is achieved in meditation, and researchers in various medical facilities have long documented the effects of such a state. In 1988, San Francisco-based cardiologist Dr. Dean Ornish incorporated meditation in his treatment program for heart patients, and documented the reversal of coronary artery disease.

What his research accomplished was to uncover the hidden physiology. With meditative technique, we can influence the subtle fluctuations occurring at the quantum level.

The most influential form of inner communication with the higher Self is meditation. We know that it clears the conscious mind, obliterates the thought process and produces the "no-mind" state necessary for inducing enlightenment.

But when we talk about concentration in meditation, we are not referring to such things as cramming for a test or merging in traffic. These are situations of *pseudo*-concentration governed by external stimuli, and are often fast-paced actions. *True* concentration only occurs in a completely relaxed state. Our minds can not reach a higher level of being unless we block the environmental distractions. As long as we are removed from most outside influences, the mind feels free to focus.

Although we are consistently bombarded by sensations, suggestions, decisions, objects, materials, and others, it is *not* the world that is confused, but it is we who live in a "confused mind." How well we filter all the incoming information depends on our level of concentration, and *awareness*. Not only do we suffer disillusionment, but discontentment as well, when we continue to react to external influences.

Like the legend goes, the buck in the Himalayan forest during mating season goes crazy trying to find out where an enticing aroma is coming from. Little does it realize that the scent is coming from his own body, and is being secreted to attract a mate. Similarly, we search for peace outside ourselves, but do not realize that our true state of happiness emanates from within.

Nicole is certainly not alone in her disillusionment with life. We are subjected to disappointments and setbacks all the time, even daily. Our lives can be full of outwardly positive things, but inside we remain unhappy.

The transient comforts of money and materials are not enough to sustain us or give us complete satisfaction. The glamour of a high-paying job or owning three expensive cars will eventually fade if there is nothing more meaningful to hold our lives together.

Upon his return to Babylonia, Alexander the Great, who had set out to conquer the world, fell ill and died before he could reach home...with one last desire. He said, "When I die, cover my whole body but leave my hands out of the shroud, with my palms open. Let the whole world see that out of all my conquests this is all I am taking with me!" So we might have access to all of the riches in the world, and still suffer. In the absence of spirituality—not to be confused with religion— we try to fill our existence by seeking more superficial means.

In 1878, Nietzsche made an observation on man and the higher self, echoing what the yogis taught thousands of years before:

"Everyone has his good day, when he finds his higher self...assess and honor a painter according to the highest vision he was able to see and portray. Some...fear their higher self because...it has a ghostly freedom of coming or staying away as it wishes; for that reason it is often called a gift of the gods, while actually everything else is a gift of the gods (of chance): this, however, is the man himself."

The higher Self is within our reach. If we invite it to become a part of our lives, we can form our own bond with the infinite energy. In a sense, yoga introduces yourself to your Self.

Yoga and meditation are the most powerful forms of inner communication with the higher Self, and to experience something quite extraordinary. In the scriptures, Psalm 46 reads, "Be still and know that I am God." The inner peace we achieve from meditation is like having a divine experience...an intoxicating and joyful state.

Meditation has been the greatest gift ever bestowed upon mankind. Thousands of years ago, the yoga masters set out to answer why has human behavior evolved from the instinctual behavior of animals?

Humans share the same urges as animals: to eat, take water, sleep, propagate the species. But our physicality and emotions are not the fundamental differences between the species. The single most important skill we possess is *concentration*, which coordinates the mind with the body. It is our ability to *focus* on the spiritual realm in spite of our needs that has led to our evolution.

Focusing our energies provides us with access to the spiritual secrets hidden from the everyday conscious mind. Yet very few of us ever train or exercise this power to know. The greater our power of concentration, the more effective we are at everything we do.

Nicole, a ninth-grade teacher, knows that the only way to retain what we learn is by having the *intention* to learn something in the first place, and then to give that subject our full *attention*.

She tells me that it is hard to tell who is concentrating and who is not, thinking that it depends more on body language. Assuming that the student intently hunched over the test is concentrating, she realizes that this is perhaps the *pseudo*-concentration I was talking about. After all, external behavior and appearances can fool us.

Nicole's outside appearance is one of composure and confidence, while inside she is mostly wrought with negative emotions. She asks me where all this negativity arises from. I tell her that a negative emotion is like a shy maiden: when you *look* at it, it disappears.

If left unattended, they create disturbance in the "inner world." To achieve calm within, we have to enter the realm beyond the mind.

Chapter Five

Taming the Shrew

For I am he
am born to tame you Kate,
And bring you from a wild Kate
to a Kate comfortable
as other household Kates.
—Petruchio to Katharina,
in Shakespeare's Taming of the Shrew

Where do negative emotions arise from in the first place? We usually blame them on others, the environment we live in, or the world in general. Criminals blame their acts on poverty and abuse, and patients blame their lung cancer on heredity or work place, only to leave my office and light a cigarette. I have seen patients who overeat themselves into obesity and fault an under-active thyroid gland.

We have mostly become a nation of people who no longer take responsibility for our own thoughts and actions. Perhaps it is because we misunderstand *why* we react negatively. Nicole and Bryan are surprised when I tell them that such negativity originates within ourselves, from the *primitive urges*.

The four inherent *urges* of self-preservation, hunger, sleep and sex often cause us mental anguish and bodily stress. They are the primary source of energy supplying power to our *emotions*, though they are not the emotions themselves. Like the antagonist Kate in

30

Shakespeare's *Taming of the Shrew*—whose vicious nature required much subduing before she could be made a suitable wife—our urges need to be tamed. We have the power to direct them; less they rule our lives.

The same four urges are *instinctive* in animals, and remain undirected. During the mating season, they copulate indiscriminately. Constantly on the lookout for danger, they are quick to fend off attacks. Most of their existence is spent replenishing their food supply, and when not hunting and killing, they sleep. Animals have no reasoning power; therefore, they are dominated by their urges.

Likewise, we experience an urge when we fear for our lives, feel starved, exhausted or are sexually attracted to someone. But the *human* intelligence has evolved beyond this instinctual habituation. We have the power of cognitive reasoning and the will of discrimination, yet we often still act out of impulse.

A primitive urge, when stimulated, generates emotional energy. Channeling this energy toward a specific goal then becomes a *desire* to fulfill an urge. All desire is thus nothing but the suffusion of emotional energy for repeat pleasure or avoidance of pain.

Desire directs our behavior: the desire to sleep motivates us to shut off the world. When we can not sleep, we become agitated and disturbed. We become preoccupied with the thought of how tired we are, and anticipate the first opportunity to sleep again.

We might *wish* for Prince Charming or *hope* to win the lottery, but we will never be *moved* to action until there is enough desire to get us going. Our motivation determines the fruit of our actions, whether they are good or bad. When we are ruled by our desires, however, we are less able to reason or make intelligent choices.

Regardless of consequence, a drug addict seeks pleasure from drugs because he or she is controlled by the urge to avoid pain. All *pleasure*, in fact, is an escape from the present *pain*. Nicole contends that there really isn't much of a difference between an addiction to "street drugs," and her own dependence on Valium. I agree that the much-prescribed tranquilizer is nothing more than another means of escape.

If we allow our urges to take over, we are soon taking drastic measures to see that no amount of change alters our lives. Those who are *unaware* fear change so much that they become "reptilian" in nature, quick to react at the slightest threat. A junkie will do anything for a "quick fix"; for example, the need for heroin might be so strong that an addict will habitually lie, steal, fight and even murder to obtain it.

Andre, a long-time heroin addict who Nicole and Bryan will eventually meet during our yoga sessions, has unsuccessfully undergone various forms of rehabilitation. After intense detoxification and/or methadone treatment, he still ended up back on the street, shooting dope. It seems that the physical component is easier to deal with than the psychological withdrawal.

Conventional methods of medicine fail to "cure" a junkie of his or her addiction, or eradicate Nicole's anxiety. Physicians seem more comfortable substituting one thing for another: methadone in place of heroin, tranquilizing drugs instead of tranquillity.

I confide that Andre has been learning yoga and meditation, with encouraging results. Such holistic therapy is successful in treating drug addicts. As they become more physically and mentally *aware*, they are able to recognize that "escape" is an uncontrolled desire to avoid pain.

Mind is a creature of habit, and once a particular object satisfies a desire, we then develop a strong emotional *attachment* to it. The danger lies in this *dependency* on the object(s) of our desire. When an object, a person or a situation satisfies our desires, our world becomes complicated.

Cars, money, property, parents, children, lovers—human beings form intense attachments, or bonds with anything that makes them feel happy, secure, fulfilled or protected. When we are conditioned by our belief systems, we feel threatened when they are disputed. But any dependency continues to create powerful negative emotions such as jealousy, greed, anger, despair and pride.

Such emotional disturbance distorts our perceptions and inhibits our creative force. On account of misdirected energy, Nicole is constantly negative.

Our perceptions of the world have become distorted because we equate happiness with *having* and *acquiring*. The less we have, the more we want, proving that satisfying desire leads to further dissatisfaction. Bryan admits that the world is too oriented around materialism.

Ask a multi-millionaire how much money is enough, and he could reply "*Just a little more.*" Life for such a person is a rat race, a futile attempt at happiness by accumulating excessive wealth.

Greed for money is no different than the need for heroin; both are dependent behaviors arising from uncontrolled urge and misdirected desire. As our capacity for reflective *awareness* enlarges significantly, we learn to postpone our needs and control our urges.

Human beings will never be *desireless*. As long as they have physical bodies, they have desires. The challenge is choosing which desires to act upon, and channeling energy constructively. When we learn to redirect this energy, we develop the power of discrimination. The role of meditation is to simply help us become better channelers, so that we are no longer slaves of our urges and desires. If we remain *unaware* of the source of our desires, emotions and habits, we will continue to suffer from painful attachments.

When we practice meditation over time, "big problems" become "non-issues," and a sense of completeness and sufficiency cultivates in us. We become aware of the four inherent urges of self-preservation, hunger, sleep and sex and develop the power to direct them.

"The Other"

Most fear originates from the idea of "the other." Separating others from ourselves accounts for our urge of self-preservation, or fear of the "unknown."

Fear is nothing more than a distortion of self-preservation, and leads to anxious preoccupation. Jean-Paul Sartre explores the fear of "the other" in *Nausea*. The protagonist Antoine Roquentin says, *"I feel so far away from them, on the top of this hill. It seems as though I belong to another species...it is their city, a good, solid, bourgeois city. They aren't afraid, they feel at home."* The character struggles so much with the existence of others that he comes to fear his own existence as well.

The learned and the fool equally fear death, each one wishing, *"May I not cease to be."* More than anything else, human beings are preoccupied by their fear of death and catastrophic illness. Our fear can depend on past experience, but often it is the intense sensory *attachment* to our physicality. The fear of this physical part of ourselves decaying or dying wreaks so much havoc on our capacities that our productive energy is wasted.

Surrendering our sensory attachments, we begin to accept that our physical selves are transitory. In the practice of daily meditation, we somewhat glimpse the face of "death." Because our senses are withdrawn, our physicality seems to "dissolve" in a spiritual *awareness*. This is why, as meditators advance in their practice, they learn to overcome the fear of death. It is actually as though these minute doses of "mini-death" desensitize us against the "final exit"!

Eat to Live, or Live to Eat?

During our lifetime we eat about the combined weight of 6 elephants! Ideally, we satisfy this urge for nourishment by eating nutritional food. But since studies show that Americans seem to be getting progressively fatter each year, it seems as if we are making unhealthy choices.

It has been estimated that people in North America are carrying around more than 200,000,000 tons of excess fat. In fact, as many as thirty percent of Americans are either overweight or clinically obese. And if we are what we eat, then most of us are compulsive and indigestible. A compulsive eater will go into a candy store, grab whatever is wrapped in a tasty package and eat it without even thinking. Overall, there is excess red meat, sugar, fat, salt and processed foods, and not enough fresh fruits and vegetables, complex carbohydrates or lean sources of protein in our diets.

When we become more *aware* of our health, we are able to discriminate between healthy and unhealthy. A person who meditates and is more discriminating might reject the nutritionally empty calories behind the seductive wrapping.

Oblivion

Too many of us are either sleep-deprived, or sleep in a disturbed state. Deep and restful sleep is vital for both our physical and mental rejuvenation. The urge to sleep might go unsatisfied for many reasons, but without sleep, we are less *aware*.

It is the *quality*, not the *quantity* of sleep that counts. We are less productive sleepers when we dream, for it is energy consuming. Unconscious material manifests itself as a dream or nightmare.

On the other hand, meditation encourages deep, dreamless sleep, and dispenses any nonessential data stored in the unconscious.

Copulate, or Procreate?

The sexual urge serves a unique function. And unlike other urges, the sexual act involves another person. Since dependence on a partner creates strong *attachments,* satisfaction becomes highly unpredictable. It is no wonder then that the sexual urge is the most fertile ground for breeding negative emotions.

Controlling the sexual urge does not necessarily mean abstaining. This only indicates making conscientious, skillful choice, rather than acting compulsively. If we react like animals every time we have a sexual desire, it becomes habitual. After all, it is the animal who *copulates*, and the human being who unites to *procreate*. Although procreation is necessary for the propagation of the species, it is not necessary for survival.

All pleasure is nothing but *concentration*. Pleasure in sex is no different. The greater the attention and *concentration* we provide for one partner, the greater the pleasure we receive. Meditating helps to develop the *concentration* necessary to divert the sexual impulse from many partners.

A large percentage of men suffer impotency, not knowing that the mind is a sex organ as well. Meditation has also been known to alleviate impotency by easing the unnecessary mental tension that prevents impotent men from enjoying sex.

The synchronicity between the mind and body during sex is culminated in the orgasm, which is entirely blissful. It is the reason why sexual energy between human beings is so sacred, thus traditionally referred to as "holy matrimony."

Chapter Six

Power Within

*There is the path of joy and there is the path
of pleasure, Both attract the soul.
The two paths lie in front of man. Pondering
on them, the wise chooses the path of joy:
the fool takes the path of pleasure.*
—Katha Upanishad

How do we translate the understanding of our inherent urges into practical wisdom? Meditation provides us with the opportunity to observe, rather than participate, in fulfilling uncontrolled desires. Exploring our inner resources, we develop a sense of mental dispassion, and a corresponding decrease in our dependency on the material world.

As observers, our perspective becomes refined, and we inculcate the power to distinguish stress from strength. By overcoming our fears, our mind becomes clear, creative and intuitive. Uncovering the latent "power within," we restore our self-confidence and gain control.

Meditation is a journey *of* the physical self *through* the mental self *to* the spiritual Self. I believe it is that, and more. Free from external influence, we experience a sense of blossoming and completeness within. Far from the pain of loneliness, the meditative art encourages a love of solitude.

Human beings will always act on their urges, but those actions can become less embedded in outside attachments through meditation. Becoming meditative frees us of our physical and mental limitations. In a sense, we will finally be able to let go. For Nicole, it may help her to reduce anxiety, clear her non-essential thoughts and achieve tranquility. I meditate daily, and I can affirm that it does provide an unlimited source of inner strength.

We know that most desires motivate our actions, and that our emotions arise from the four primitive urges. Some desires, however, stem from higher *awareness*, like unconditional *love* or altruism. The sage Shantideva once said,

> Whatever joy there is in the world
> All comes from desiring others to be happy,
> And whatever suffering there is in the world
> All comes from desiring myself to be happy.

In its pure form, love is selfless and sacrificial. The more loving we are, the less limited we become in our reactions toward others. After all, selfishness, or ego-centeredness is the sole cause of loneliness. There are people who are so wrapped up in themselves that their capacity to empathize with others is terribly small.

The most positive, powerful emotion is love. It is ideally why two people enter into a relationship with each other, and the reason why Nicole and Bryan are planning to get married.

Spontaneously, the heart experiences *joy*, which is another source of "power within." Children effortlessly reflect the *innocence* and joy in life that we, as adults, want so much to attain or recapture. Watch the spontaneous actions of a toddler. He or she is delighted by something as simple as a cloud in the sky, or a ladybug on the sidewalk.

Joy is best when it happens out of the blue, and the same is true of

Joy is best when it happens out of the blue, and the same is true of laughter. We laugh at a joke because the punch line is so unexpected. As adults, we can increase our joy simply by laughing more often. It is, of course, the best medicine and antidote for stress. We miss the punch line when we impose *expectations* on our lives. Instead of letting joy happen naturally, we create stress for ourselves and suffer.

When we lose our expectations, we experience joy and become *tranquil*. In such a state of mind, we become undisturbed by things beyond our control, and develop more self-acceptance.

If we remain unaware, and our self-esteem is low, we lose the *will* to strive for the better. Instead, we more easily succumb to desires. Becoming vulnerable, we end up letting undesirable people and situations take control over our lives. Due to this absence of will, we are conflicted, unhappy and further enslaved by our urges and desires.

"Then how do we develop the knowledge that enables us to take control of our lives?" Nicole wants to know.

I believe that from personal experience, there is no method more complete than meditation. Immersed in such a positive state, we are beyond the judgments of others, and become non-judgmental ourselves.

Meditation unfolds our power within. Freeing us from our *dependencies*, fears and self-hatred, it "tames the shrews" that nibble away at our positive attributes. Our innermost core Self *is* reachable once we embark upon the meditative journey. When the path becomes familiar, we return again and again...and take with us the positive emotions of *love, joy, tranquility* and *will* as souvenirs.

But before I venture with Nicole and Bryan on their own meditative journey, we first must delve into the mysteries of the mind.

Chapter Seven

Subtle Body

Some flesh to eat,
a beautiful woman,
and a corpse-
So the same body is seen three ways,
by a wolf,
a passionate youth,
and a yogi.
—a Sanskrit verse

In my explorations, I have come to know the Spirit as the wizard, the mind, or *subtle body*, as the magic wand and the *physical body* as the magic or illusion. What we find in the subtle realm are all the qualities present in the *gross body*, but magnified to their maximum potential.

According to yoga philosophy, the complete human organism consists of the *Purusha*, also called the pure Self, or Spirit. This individual Self is the part of us that is closest to the Universal Reality, though it remains hidden by the other "superficial" entities that make up a human being.

The innermost covering of the soul or pure Self, is the *karana sharira*, or *causal body*—the "knower." Its immediate envelope is the *sukshma sharira*, or *subtle body*—the "mind"—and the outermost cloak is the *sthula sharira*, or *gross body*.

The *physical body*—the realm of matter that is under the influence of time, space and causation, and is subject to *entropy* and death—has long been understood. It perishes at death, but the subtle and causal sheaths are carried forth through countless lifetimes.

Bound within the subtle and causal levels, the *everfree, everpure, everwise awareness* of the individual Spirit becomes trapped within the cycle of birth and death.

This really sparks Nicole's imagination, and she begs me to elaborate.

"I've always been fascinated by past lives, future lives, you name it. How did the yogis come to understand the concept?" she asks.

Bryan is more doubtful. The existence of *reincarnated* energy is harder to comprehend than the scientific evidence of *universal* energy. His natural skepticism is belied by growing interest, so he urges me to go on.

I give Bryan an analogy: our *physical body* is like the computer *hardware*, and the *software* is the *subtle body*. The "artificial intelligence" of the software can be downloaded from one system to another through cyberspace, and thus "reincarnate," actually coming into a new "body." Similarly, the "natural intelligence" can transmigrate and remanifest.

So the subtle and causal bodies act as a home to the Spirit. If our body and mind work together, why doesn't the *subtle body* die with the physical one?

In order to comprehend the process of reincarnation, we have to understand the sequence of evolution, to know how these coverings evolve in the first place.

The *causal body* is the field of "I" *awareness* which is in close proximity to the pure Self, and is the expression of the blissful, dream-less sleep state and the realm of meditation.

It is the *subtle body*, or the "global mind" that remains a mystery. Scientists are still asking themselves the same questions the yogis did thousands of years ago: How can we prove the existence of the mind when we can not see it? What exactly is contained in the mind?

This *subtle body*—the second layer of the human cake—is made of several ingredients: *I-consciousness, intellect, ego, mind*, the *five cognitive senses*, the *five faculties of action* and their *psychological correlates*. The *subtle body* corresponds to the dream state, and we find it hard to perceive that it even exists.

Our mind—that magic wand—is invisible to the naked eye, and is composed of both an *internal* and *external instrument*. What we re-fer to as the *internal instrument* has four ingredients: the *individual consciousness, intellect, ego* and the logical, linear thinking *mind*.

The *chitta*, or *individual consciousness*, is our limited reflection of the pure Self. We are one part of the whole universe, but we often acknowledge only our own reality or what immediately surrounds us. From such a limited viewpoint, the world seems to revolve around us. From the universal vantagepoint, we revolve with the world.

The *subtle body* is linked to the *causal body* through the *buddhi*, or *intellect*. It represents our translogical, intuitive comprehension, and is also the storehouse of conscious memory, as well as the *samskaras*, or our unconscious, subliminal impressions. When we need to recall information while taking a test, we call upon the intellect to give us the appropriate responses.

The *subtle body*, also home to the *ahankara* or *ego*, is known as the "Chief Executive Officer" of the mind. This "false identification" is prompted by our subconscious impulses, and seeks out experi-ences in the world which satisfy them.

42

The ego-self often serves as the source of our mental afflictions and emotional troubles. The *ego*, or "CEO," regularly forgets who the real President of the company is—the pure Self—and likes to run the show according to its own rules.

Directly derived from the *intellect*, the "CEO" handpicks what it likes and dislikes in the world, and makes the necessary arrangements with the memory banks. The *ego* is an entirely thought-bound entity, conditioned by the need to preserve its own pseudo-existence. If we want to be considered by others as intelligent, our ego-self will seek out situations and relationships in which we seem superior. Perhaps our physical appearance is important, and the *ego* will confine itself to times and places in which we outshine others.

Out of the *ego* emerges the concept of linear thinking *mind*, or *manas*. It serves the *ego* by coordinating the functions of the senses and faculties. It sorts, labels and classifies enormous everyday sensory data, and also works closely with the *intellect* and the *ego* in the decision-making process.

Our *consciousness*, our *intellect*, our *mind* and our *ego* all act together. Collectively, they comprise the inner psychic shell overlying the pure Self. Forming the innermost center of our personality, this deeply conditioned instrument seems to control us more than we control it.

Contained in the *subtle body* are also the *potentials* for ten faculties of both perception and action. They are labeled the *external instrument*, because they function outwardly. Our *five cognitive senses* of perception are hearing, sight, smell, taste and touch, and their corresponding physical organs: the ears, eyes, nose, tongue and skin. Also found in the *subtle body* are the *five faculties of action:* the power of speech, grasping, motion, reproduction and excretion, and their corresponding organs—the tongue, hands, feet, genitals and rectum. The senses and faculties are connected to the gross matter through their physical counterparts.

43

The *internal instrument* interprets what we receive and assimilate through the *external instrument*. It is our mind, or the *subtle body* that operates directly through the ten faculties, and is the link between the *external* and the *internal instrument*.

As invisible as ether, the *subtle body* is an air-like medium, which remains unseen to the naked eye. Radio, television and X-rays were once unseen phenomenon until developing technology unveiled them. As far as ether is concerned, advancing technology is still in the developmental stages, though scientists hope to soon make the higher energy field visible for study.

Considerable evidence suggests that a holographic energy template, or *subtle body*, exists associated with our *physical body*. And the "etheric interface" the *subtle body* makes with the physical one has been proven scientifically in various experiments. (Fig.4)

In the 1940's, neuroanatomist at Yale University named Harold S. Burr mapped the shape of the electrical fields during salamander embryogenesis. He discovered this field by injecting ink into the unfertilized egg's axial region. He found that the newborn salamanders possessed an energy field roughly shaped like the adult animal.

He conducted further research with tiny seedlings, and again found that the electrical field around a sprout was not the shape of the original seed. Instead, it resembled the adult plant that it would someday become. Burr's accumulative data suggested that both the developing animal and plant organism is destined to follow a prescribed growth template, and that such a plate was then deter-mined by the organism's individual electromagnetic field.

A unique experiment recorded by electrophotography—the "phantom leaf effect"—also provides evidence of the *subtle body*. An electrophotograph of a partially amputated leaf surprisingly reveals a picture of the whole, intact leaf. The amputated portion still ap-

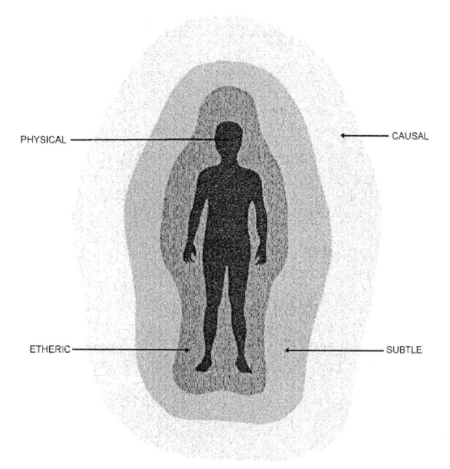

FIGURE 4. HUMAN BIO-ENERGETIC FIELD

pears in the photograph, even though the missing fragment has been physically destroyed.

Scientist Allen Detrick showed the phantom trick on both sides of the leaf, displaying the three-dimensional spatial and organizational nature of such a bio-energetic field—one that is holographic in nature. By the same process, I. Dumitrescu, a Romanian scientist, cut a circular hole in a leaf and produced a *leaf within a leaf*, also confirming the holographic nature of energy fields that surround all living things.

45

The subtle energy template that encases our physical matter is *never* subject to decay. The "phantom pain" experienced by an amputee also explains the existence of a residual energy template. Even after a limb is removed, patients report sensation or pain in the area where the now-amputated body part once existed!

The pioneer of Kirlian photography, Russian scientist Semyon Kirlian photographed living organisms in the presence of a high frequency, high voltage and low amperage electrical field. When a piece of the photographic film is interposed between the object and the electrode, a spark discharge pattern called a "corona" is captured on film. It gets its name from the outer corona of the sun during an eclipse. Kirlian confirmed Burr's measurements of the salamander, translating them into the visual characteristics of an electrical "corona" discharge.

Similarly, the marriage of computer technology to the X-ray has produced the CT Scanner, which can also provide previously invisible images of electrical energy fields—this time in humans. The PET (Positive Emission Tomography) emits a two-dimensional picture of a human energy field; in addition, it gives information about cellular function. The MRI (Magnetic Resonance Imaging) opens yet another window on the body. This time, it yields even more detailed cellular pictures of organ structure and function. MRI capitalizes on the magnetic properties of the body's "etheric interface" energy system...the same system that the yogis uncovered thousands of years ago without all this fancy equipment!

In meditation, they opened their "divine eye," and decoded the microcosmic hologram. Scientists in the next millenium will prove and discover the same unseen connection. The next great step in technology might certainly lie in the creation of a CT or MRI scanner that would image the *subtle body*! Such a scanner might someday detect illness at the subtle level before the disease manifests, making it true preventive medicine.

Dr. William Tiller, a professor of material science at Stanford University and a leader in the field of subtle energies, described the first frequency model of our bio-energetic fields. He divided the mental body into three different levels: the "instinctive," the "intellectual" and the "spiritual." Interestingly, Tiller's model parallels yoga philosophy. The "astral," the "instinctive" and the "intellectual" bodies correspond to the *subtle body*, while the "spiritual" body correlates to the *causal body*. Through the "etheric interface," the *physical body* is linked to the *subtle body*. Each of these subtle bodies has a bell-shaped curve distribution of energies. (Fig. 5)

These subtle energy bodies act as vehicles of containment for our mobile *awareness*.Our *awareness* dances like waves in the ocean. Upon awakening, the wave of *awareness* ascends into the *gross body*. In the dream world, the wave disappears within the *subtle body*. The wave comes to a standstill during the deep, dreamless

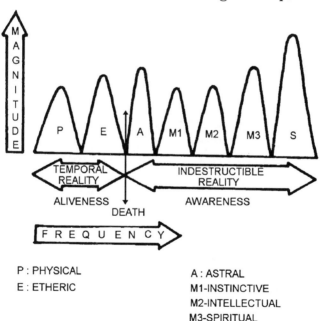

P : PHYSICAL

E : ETHERIC

A : ASTRAL

M1-INSTINCTIVE

M2-INTELLECTUAL

M3-SPIRITUAL

S : SPIRIT

FIGURE 5. HUMAN BIO-ENERGETIC SPECTRUM

(Based on a model by W. Tiller, Ph.D.)

sleep state in the realm of the *causal body*.

What we see is only the *reflection,* and not the final *realization.* During deep sleep, we barely touch the source. We continuously fall back into the experiences of the dream and waking states, which can occur like tidal waves that destroy the mirrored reflection of the pure Self.

The physical form cannot exist without the energizing nourishment and spatial guidance of the "etheric interface." When our physical bodies are born, they are cradled in an invisible net—the spatial outline of a human being—which surrounds us until our death.

Because the *physical body* and "etheric interface" are so interwoven and interdependent, they form what Tiller refers to as the *Human Temporal Reality.*

Human Temporal Reality, or *aliveness,* refers to the earth-bound time frame of reference, and our own physical perspective of reality. Under the influence of time, space, causation and gravity, it is therefore subject to decay, or *positive* entropy.

Human Indestructible Reality, or *awareness,* refers to the non-physical, non-space, and non-time level of existence. The subtle energetic bodies beyond the "etheric interface" are indestructible, and demonstrate *negative* entropy.

The frequencies of the *subtle* and *causal bodies* are so *supraluminal* that they fall in the domain of *negative* time, *negative* space and *negative* entropy. Tiller utilized Einstein's equation that predicts the existence of *faster-than-light* energy, which has magneto-electrical properties. These subtle energies are not easily measurable by conventional means, since the human limit stops short at the speed of light—186,000 miles per second!

Energy can *never* be created or destroyed, only transformed, and thus *always* remains constant. At the time of death, or *excarnation*, the energy link of *prana* or *aliveness* between the *subtle* and the *gross body* is severed. This *aliveness*, or kinetic energy, is returned to the free energy of the universe, and the *gross body* to the elements.

Yet the entire energy field of *awareness* shifts from the *physical* to the *subtle* and *causal bodies,* and comes to a quintessence. As a panorama of memories, the entire life experience flashes forth "all at once" at the moment of death. This "life review"—completed in an instant of *earthly* time—has been reported in near-death experience. This reminds me of Dr. Raymond Moody's accounts of patient's near-death experiences. Amazingly, each and every one of them who claimed such an experience reported "seeing the light," a "being" of light that was indescribably brilliant and comforting.

The *awareness* then encapsulates this "light," or the pure Self, transmigrating only to reincarnate. This explains the "circle of life," and how we are ultimately influenced by our previous subliminal impressions, or memories—contained in the *subtle* and *causal bodies*—which are "carried over" from life cycle to life cycle. This *awareness*, or potential energy is thus an ever-evolving continuum.

Between death and rebirth, it is the memory, or the thought content within the subtle and causal plane that *creates* "heaven" or "hell" for the departed soul. There is no physical existence of heaven or hell as such; each is merely a state of mind. After all, man has explored the galaxies and has not heard angelic music yet, and fathomed the deep seas only to discover oil!

The entire lifetime experience(s) is contained within the *subtle body*. It is our durable *subtle body* that contains timeless, spaceless circles of indestructible energy. Through our thoughts, actions, and behaviors, we can either fortify or nourish these vortices of inner intelligence, or we can undernourish and contaminate the information that is "carried over."

49

The total algebraic sum of all present and past experiences deter-mines the vector, or direction of the transmigrating body. The kind of compatible "fertilized field" that it enters—for its next incarna-tion—will depend on the *quality* of its contents.

The union of the egg or ovum with the sperm generates this "fertil-ized field." The holographic "mother thought body" surrounding the ovum joins with the holographic "father thought body" around the sperm as well. But only when the "migrating thought body"—the encapsulated transmigrating soul in the subtle and causal realm—unites with the "fertilized field," *conception* occurs and true growth begins.

As a result, the physical and mental attributes of the offspring are *never* the perfect algebraic sum of the mother and the father. There is always a *third* element. It is really a union of three, not two, that defines life.

Though intrigued by the information, Bryan wonders why, if rein-carnation is valid, does the world population fluctuate. To belie some of his remaining doubts, I provide him with an analogy, and scientific evidence. In my way of thinking, reincarnation explains the "unexplained."

In an ocean, each wave is analogous to the individual lifetime, as if the crest is birth, and the trough is death. The number of waves—like the world's population—vary at different times, yet the ocean itself—like the energy of *awareness*—remains constant.

Uncovering the mystery of reincarnation, Dr. Ian Stevenson, a pro-fessor of psychiatry at the University of Virginia Medical School, has done extensive research in the past thirty years. He has col-lected and analyzed over two thousand cases of children with rein-carnation-type memories and experiences from all over the world. For instance, many of them exhibited xenoglossy, the ability to speak a language to which they were never exposed.

A person's previous incarnation apparently has a direct influence on that same person's current *physical body*. For instance, a boy who had shot himself in the head in a former life was reported as having two scars which perfectly lined up in exactly the same place as the bullet's entry and exit wounds. Another boy, with a reddish-mark across his neck, recalled having his throat slit in a previous life. Similarly, a young man had a birthmark that resembled a surgical scar in the exact location he had had surgery in a past life. In fact, Dr. Stevenson in some cases, has been able to obtain hospital and/or autopsy records of the deceased persons. By this, he has correlated the *exact* location of present birthmarks or deformities with injuries in the past experience of such individuals.

He also reports of Burmese children recalling their former lives as United States Air Force pilots who were shot down over Burma during the Second World War. Coincidentally, they were fairer in both complexion and hair color than their siblings.

Dr. Stevenson concluded that by acting as a holographic template, the energy field carries past information between lifetimes on an "extended body." He thus provides confirmatory evidence for both Dr. Tiller's theory and yoga philosophy.

Excellent overview by Edgar Mitchell, writings of Professor C. J. Ducasse of Brown University, and ESP data from Duke University lend further credence to the subject. Libraries are stacked with this research and literature, though few hardly venture to know about it, or realize that it is even available.

To Nicole and Bryan, I have explained reincarnation with powerful, scientific validation. Awed that such a seemingly mystical and esoteric belief could be so simple, straightforward and logical, they became convinced that the possibility of "life after life" certainly exists.

Chapter Eight

Wheels of Awareness

The Wheel of the Year turns on and on, bringing us
to and from each season, and from and to another. What will be is. What was will be. All time is
here and now inside this sacred space.
—from traditional Celtic Sabbat ritual

Throughout pagan tradition—from the Norse, Teutonic and Celtic practices to those of Roman and Greek origins—all ritual was performed within a circle. Practitioners visualized pouring energy as a blue-white light into a circle. Providing protection from imagined demons and evil spirits, the circle stored the generated energy until it could be directed outward.

Before taking place in a Sabbat ritual, pagans purified themselves of all negative influences by anointing each of their "energy centers": the genitals, the navel, between the breasts, the throat, the forehead and the top of the head. Only then could positive energies be invoked.

Thousands of years ago, when old world pagans had yet to don ceremonial robes, the ancient yogis were transmitting higher energies within the seven special centers of consciousness. These *chakras*, or centers of consciousness resemble whirling vortices of subtle energies and play a vital role in the regulation of various states of *awareness*.

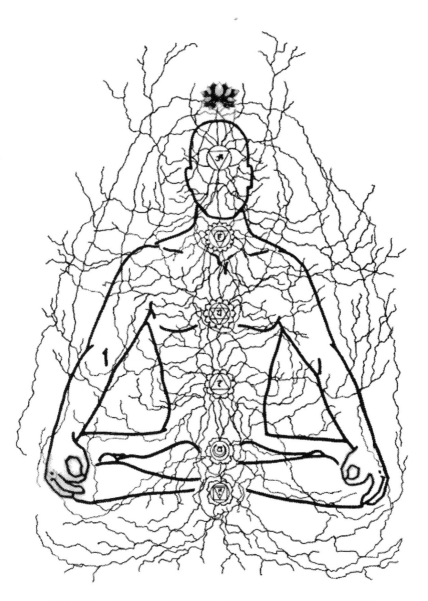

FIGURE 6. CHAKRA AND NADI SUBTLE ENERGY NETWORK

Situated in the *subtle body*, the seven *chakras* are in the "same latitude" as certain parts of the *physical body*. They ascend from the base of the spine to the crown of the head.

The *chakras* are connected to each other, and to portions of the physical cellular structure through subtle energy channels known as *nadis*. Formed by fine threads of subtle energetic matter, the *nadis* represent an extensive network of fluid-like energies, which parallel the bodily nerves, though they are not the arteries, veins or nerves themselves. Because of the intricate interconnection with the nerve plexus and a special alignment with the endocrine glands, the *nadis* affect the nature and quality of nerve transmission and create changes in cells via the hormonal link. Various sources indicate that the yogis deciphered up to 72,000 or more *nadis* or etheric channels in the subtle anatomy of human beings! (Fig.6)

The three main channels or *nadis* are the *sushumna*, the *ida* and the *pingala*. They originate at the base of the spine and travel upwards, throughout the body. The *sushumna nadi* is centrally located, and winds its way along the spinal canal. At the "level" of the larynx, it is divided into the anterior portion and the posterior division, both terminating in the ventricular cavity of the brain. The *ida* and the *pingala* nadis also travel along the spinal column, and retire in the respective left and right nostrils. During their course, the three main *nadis* crisscross each other at the *chakras*.

"Is there a way to prove this?" Bryan asks me. I reply that it is particularly amazing that the ancient description of *nadis* and *chakras* resembles the modern anatomical layout of the nerves and plexuses. Not one yogi ever dissected a physical body, and even if they had, such dissection would be futile, since the *nadis* and *chakras* are invisible! However, by mapping *prana* through introspective experimentation, they discovered this subtle energy network. The flow of *prana* is the subtle counterpart of the physical nerve impulse. It is this unseen connection of the *chakras* to the *physical body* that is the secret to our health and vitality.

54

Each major *chakra* has its own specific frequency of vibrational energy. The *chakras* translate energy of a higher dimensional nature into neuro-hormonal output and thus act as *transformers*. Involving the flow of higher energies, these multi-dimensional centers have their own particular psychic and physical function. Each communicates with the cells through the nervous and endocrine system, producing neuro-hormonal reactions affecting our moods and behavior. The field of Psycho-neuro-immunology echoes the existence of *chakras*, and the deeper connections between the brain, the endocrine glands and the immune system.

In Japan, Dr. Hiroshi Motoyama took multiple electrical recordings of *chakras* from a number of advanced meditators. When the subjects claimed that a particular *chakra* had been "awakened," an electrode that was placed over the designated area recorded a greater amplitude and frequency of the electrical field. This was significantly greater than the energy recorded from the *chakras* of subjects in the control group. Motoyama replicated this phenomenon many times over the years.

The Russian-born researcher Itzhak Bentov duplicated Motoyama's findings, using similar equipment to prove the emission of potential, electrostatic energy from the *chakras*.

Furthermore, Dr. Valarie Hunt at UCLA demonstrated the presence of high frequency *chakra* oscillations never before reported in scientific literature. The normal frequency range of brain waves is between 0-100 cycles/second, with the most information generated between 0-30 cycles/second. The frequency of muscle goes up to 225 cycles/second and that of the heart up to 250 cycles/second. In contrast, the readings from the *chakras* lay in a band of accelerated frequencies between 100-1600 cycles/second—higher than anything that has ever been recorded from the human body. This high frequency is in fact a *subharmonic* of an original *chakra* signal which is in the range of many thousands cycles/second.

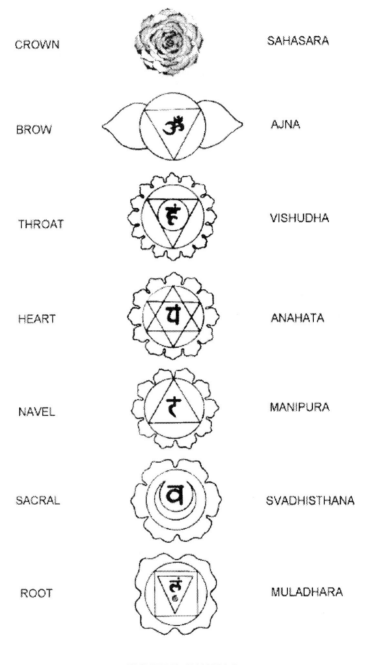

CROWN   SAHASARA

BROW   AJNA

THROAT   VISHUDHA

HEART   ANAHATA

NAVEL   MANIPURA

SACRAL   SVADHISTHANA

ROOT   MULADHARA

FIGURE 7. CHAKRAS

Dr. Hunt also utilized the talents of Rosilyn Bruyere, a trained psychic clairvoyant while electronically monitoring the *chakras* by EMG electrodes. While observing the subject's subtle energy, or "auric field"—rings of color surrounding the bodies of living things—Bruyere was denied immediate feedback of the electrical activity. Dr. Hunt found that the clairvoyant's observation of the "auric fields" correlated with the electrode recordings. Each color was associated with a different EMG wave pattern at the *chakra* level. For instance, when Bruyere described one subject's aura as red, the monitor displayed the red wave pattern.

Each *chakra* is also represented by a specific color, an exact shape and a corresponding, resonant *mantra,* the syllabic vibration utilized in the technique of advanced meditation.

In yoga literature, the *chakras* are visualized as beautiful lotus flowers. (Fig.7) The roots are symbolic of the fine, delicate *nadis* that distribute nourishment. The *chakras* disperse the vital life force and energy into the *physical body*...from root to limb to highest branch.

The *first* and lowest *chakra*, called the *"root"* or *muladhara,* is located near the tailbone or the base of the spine. Composed of just four lotus petals, its cosmic power lies in solidity and groundedness, like the sitting still in meditation. Its psychological correlates are the sense of smell, the element of Earth and the color yellow. Taking the shape of a circle containing a square and a downward-pointing triangle, its mantra is *Lam.*

The *second* sacral *chakra*, or the *svadhisthana,* (*"own abode"*) is located at the level of the sexual organs. This *chakra* has six petals, represents the elements of water and taste, and is both cleansing and sexual in nature. Its color is pure white, is the shape of a circle containing a crescent moon, and has the mantra *Vam.*

Near the navel and around the solar plexus is the *third chakra*, or *manipura.* (*"filled with jewels"*) It is like our own miniature sun of bright-red heat energy, and fire and sight represent it. As a lotus, it has ten petals, takes the shape of a circle containing a triangle, and has the intonation *Ram.*

Located at the chest center is the *fourth chakra*, or *anahata* (*"unstruck sound"*). The corresponding element is air because of its association with the heart and lungs, which circulate oxygen throughout the body. This *chakra* displays twelve lotus petals, and is epitomized by the Solomon's Seal, or the Star of David. The two geometrically super-imposed triangles (one pointing down, the other pointing upward) represent the transition between the first three *chakras* (lower) and the last three (higher). The gray color of ether, the sensation of touch and the mantra *Yam* also represent the heart *chakra.*

The *fifth chakra*, or *vishuddha* (*"space"*) is located at the level of the throat. Associated with speech and hearing, it is more ether than air. It is a sixteen-petaled lotus, and is golden-white in color. Taking the shape of a circle containing a triangle, enclosing in turn a smaller circle, its mantra is *Hum.*

Ajna, the *sixth chakra* of *wisdom*, is located between the eyebrows. The yogis refer to this center as the "third eye of man," as it is the seat of intuition and the subtle organ of clairvoyance (literally, "clear vision."). Its element is *mahant*, meaning *"majesty"* or *"greatness,"* for it transcends the previous *chakras*. A two-petaled lotus flower in the shape of a white circle containing a triangle, its intonation is *Om.*

The *seventh chakra* bears the name *sahasara*, or *"thousand-rayed."* The final *chakra* has no corresponding element, color or sound because the Absolute Self that governs it is beyond all quality. Situated at the crown of the head, it is a lotus flower of a thousand petals radiating splendor.

The energy that activates the *chakras* and assists in the awakening of higher *awareness* is called *kundalini.* It is described as a "coiled serpent" which lies dormant at the first major *chakra* but is ever poised to spring into action. In most individuals, this energy remains unexplored or dormant.

In each individual, the potential energy of *awareness* is polarized: the positive (+) polarity at the *sahasara*, or crown, and the negative (-) polarity *kundalini* lying dormant at the base of the spine. We only utilize a fraction of *kundalini* energy, when in fact there is an infinite reservoir which lies uncovered. The abundant power of this energy is not even imagined by "official" science!

There are individuals who possess an abundance of energy, insight, and creativity. History provides testimony of dynamic geniuses and "miracle" performers of every age and culture. People attribute their seemingly "otherworldy" talents and perceptions to such things as psychokinesis, "ESP," telepathy, astral-travel or other supernatural, even religious phenomena. Yet, what they do not realize is that such individuals have learned to unleash the latent power of *kundalini* energy within. In fact, what they have accessed is the unconscious world.

The *kundalini* power contains latent memories—both personal and transpersonal—and our way of understanding it is in terms of the unconscious.

When its power is unleashed in a coordinated fashion, as in structured meditation, the serpentine *kundalini* energy dances slowly up the spinal column as a wave of beauty and bliss. Along the way, it awakens the half-asleep buds of the *chakras*, and the lotus flowers begin to blossom.

Sir John Woodroffe eloquently describes this blossoming: When *Shakti*, the feminine *kundalini* power is asleep, one is *awake* to the external world. When she awakens to unite with the masculine *sahasara* or *Shiva* at the crown, then one is *asleep* to the world, and immersed in pure *awareness*.

Nowhere can the union of *Shakti* and *Shiva* be more beautifully understood, however, than in a work of art. As illustrated on the cover of this book by artist PennyLea Morris Seferovich, the meaning of the feminine *kundalini Shakti*—represented in the "half-moon"—and the masculine *sahasara* or *Shiva*—designated by the two "eye dots"—culminates in the meeting of the soul.

These two forces transcend both the physical body, which is represented by the square, and the mind field, which is likened to the circle, to become the unified spirit of one.

As a potential power, *kundalini* sustains ordinary *awareness*, but when she unites with *sahasara*, she ascends to a state of higher, or pure *awareness*. Her ascent embodies the process of evolution in which we as human beings come to realize our full *potential*.

This energy unravels within us like a flowing river, providing us with a constant source of inner power. In Gita Mehta's *A River Sutra*, the bureaucrat who has retired by the river, says that, *"In the silence of the ebbing night, I sometimes think I can hear the river's heartbeat pulsing under the ground before she reveals herself at last to the anchorites of Shiva deep in meditation..."*

It is told that the divine *Shiva*, or the *Creator and Destroyer of Worlds*, blessed the river and named it *Narmada*, or *Delightful One*. With her eternal and inexhaustible energy, the river symbolizes the dance between the human and the divine, much like the *kundalini* unwinds the energy that is both personal and universal.

As the undulating energy enters its final abode, (near the "third eye" and crown) a sensation of light floods the meditative being, or microcosm. It is a beautiful union, quite like the marriage between the masculine *sahasara* energy and the feminine *kundalini* energy. There is then an infinite expansion of *awareness*...and the dance begins.

Chapter Nine

Broken Wheels

We affirm that in accordance with the Universe
we connect with the flow of energy, love, and fruitfulness,
and we release fear, judgment and negativity
in order to create sacred space for life.
—from ancient Wiccan spell,
for connecting to the cosmic flow

For 18 months, prominent psychiatrist Dr. Brian Weiss worked with a young patient named Catherine, who suffered from constant anxiety, panic attacks, phobias, insomnia and nightmares. When conventional therapy failed, he tried hypnosis. In a series of tape-recorded sessions, Catherine entered a trance state, exhibiting xenoglossy or speaking in languages that were previously unknown and recalling "past-life" memories that had contributed to her problems. Consequently, her latent fears and phobias could surface, and finally be dispensed with.

From the "spiritual plane," she could act as a conduit for information to reveal the secrets and wisdom of life and death. In just a few sessions, Catherine's symptoms disappeared, and she resumed her life—at peace once and for all. As recorded in "Many Lives, Many Masters," Dr. Weiss's first true experience with past-life changed both his and Catherine's life forever.

Genetic memory requires the unbroken passage of genetic material from generation to generation. In this case, Catherine gives

accounts of having lived many lives all over the earth, so her genetic line was repeatedly disrupted. Her past life experiences
ranged from prehistoric times, to ancient Egypt, to modern day.
From life to life, how were her memories then continued? There
was no body and certainly no genetic material, and yet she still
remembered.

During embryogenesis, the subtle energy template acts as a blueprint for the human body, and it is where the *chakras* are formed.
Each *chakra* is directly affected by the energies that are "carried
over" from its previous lives; this incarnating soul, or newborn, is
influenced by past desires, instincts, actions, behaviors and deeds.

The indestructible subtle body is an accumulation of many lifetime experiences. Each time a person's particular "cycle" returns
again to birth, it is "reviewed" so it can determine what kind of
human being it will become. For example, an individual like Mother
Theresa is most likely to *evolve*, and one like Adolf Hitler would
devolve, in the cycle of life.

Yoga associates what has occurred in a person's past lifetimes with
the *function* or *dysfunction* of chakras. Wellness or illness first starts
in this energy dimension, and is later manifested in the *physical
body*. This hidden physiology is the force behind the physical body.

If our energy field is distorted—if these circles are gradually diminished and broken altogether—physical disease soon follows. This
explains why some people seem immune to ill health while others
are subject to disease.

"Does this also explain my emotional negativity?" Nicole inquires.

While the translation between past and present occur at the *chakra*
level, our quality of life is also influenced by what we *acquire* from
day to day. In order to apply the principles of reincarnation to our
illness or wellness—to understand the "cycle of life"—it is first es-

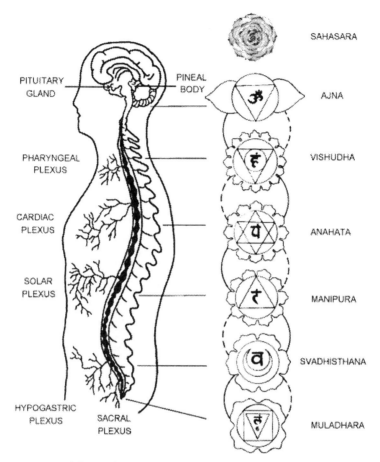

PITUITARY
GLAND

PINEAL
BODY

SAHASARA

AJNA

PHARYNGEAL
PLEXUS

VISHUDHA

CARDIAC
PLEXUS

ANAHATA

SOLAR
PLEXUS

MANIPURA

SVADHISTHANA

HYPOGASTRIC
PLEXUS

SACRAL
PLEXUS

MULADHARA

FIGURE 8. NERVE PLEXUSES AND CHAKRAS

sential to know what is contained in these seven circular wheels of *awareness.* (Fig.8)

Root Chakra

As the name indicates, the root center reflects our connectedness to the Earth, or how grounded we are. The root is the seat of the *kundalini*, and concerns our physical existence. Psychologically speaking, it is linked to our basic, primitive survival instincts, like fear of injury or bodily harm. When integrated, it can provide us with a sense of stability and security. When we feel threatened, our root *chakra* activates the "flight or fight response" mechanism, so that we are better prepared for crisis or danger.

Overactivity, however, may manifest negatively as insecurity, irrational or phobic fear, paranoia and anxiety. With too much energy invested here, a person may become fearful, over-anxious and defensive.

At the root center, accumulated stress is released, and the associated physical organs of excretion—the rectum, anal canal and urethra—symbolize the process of release.

The sacral *chakra* is closely associated with the root *chakra*, as they both refer to the processes of digestion and elimination. Dysfunction in the two lower *chakras* may indicate an inability to release or let go, and the corresponding physical ailments of constipation, irritable bowel syndrome, colon cancer and even Freudian anal fixation.

The root *chakra* is also linked with the reproductive functions of the sperm and ovum. Cosmic, creative *kundalini* potential emanating from the root *chakra* is both procreative and artistic in nature. The energy used to create new life is the same as for creating poetry, art and music. Incidentally, both infertility and lack of expression may be associated with this *chakra* dysfunction.

Sacral Chakra

Linked to the element of water, this *chakra* is the subtle seat of sexuality, and the release of bodily fluids. It is associated with the gonadal energies in the leydig cells within the testes and ovaries, and hormone production.

The sacral *chakra* involves complex sensual emotions of love and attentiveness, as well as sexual expression. Over focusing on sexuality spares little energy for higher pursuits or other types of creativity. Individuals whose energies are centered primarily in this *chakra* will tend to only seek out sexual relationships, and view others as nothing more than sexual objects.

Ailments and illnesses resulting from such dysfunction may include gynecological problems in women, bladder tumors, lower back pain, colitis, prostatitis, cancer of the cervix and other reproductive organs, and sexually transmitted disease.

Navel Chakra

The navel or solar plexus *chakra* supplies nutritive subtle energy to most of the major digestive organs, including the stomach, the large intestine, pancreas, liver, gall bladder, and adrenal glands. The food burns in the digestive oven, and the process releases active energy throughout the body. Unregulated and improper digestion is destructive, in that it contributes to upset stomach, heartburn and ulcers.

The navel *chakra* influences the amount of control we have over our lives, and can be a source of dynamic energy. Because it is linked to personal power, it can either be a source of confidence and contentment, or disillusionment, discontent and jealousy.

The source of all anger is frustrated desire or feeling powerless. Abnormal functioning of this *chakra* not only manifests in short temper and abusive behavior, but also creates inner conflict. Some psychological studies of ulcer patients reveal that they often take on too many dominant responsibilities even though they view themselves as incapable. In this way, they alternate between dominance and submission.

The solar plexus *chakra* is also closely connected to the adrenal glands, which play an important role in times of stress. Weakness, easy fatigue and vulnerability to infection and disease set in when there is blockage in this *chakra*.

The inner need for control may stem from an imbalance in the *chakra*, and on a physical level, diabetic experiences a loss of personal power when they become insulin-dependent. Metaphorically expressed it is as if the sweetness has gone out of life.

Heart Chakra

This transitional *chakra* mediates between the three lower, earthly energies and the three higher, spiritual energies. At the heart *chakra*—the center of equilibrium—these two "worlds" meet and converge. As the element of air, the fourth *chakra* is said to occupy the space between heaven and earth.

I explain to Nicole that our negative emotions arise out of the root, sacral and solar plexus *chakras*, since they are more primitive in nature. These centers below the diaphragm are primarily concerned with physical desires. By integrating our *awareness* at the heart *chakra*, we become more enlightened.

This *chakra* is our emotional center, relating to our interactions with other people. A wave of energy sweeps over the heart when we experience strong, positive feelings toward another person. This sensation may manifest in feeling "swept off our feet" when we fall in love. An open-heart *chakra* is integral to our ability to express compassion, unconditional love and altruism.

Epitomized by the bond between mother and child, the breasts are located at the level of this *chakra*, and are the only organs dedicated to the nurturence of another being. Developing compassion and empathy for others is a consequence of loving, and being loved in turn. We cultivate the sense that the world does not revolve around us completely, and that there are others to consider.

Blockages in the heart *chakra* may derive from an inability to love or regard others, and also arises from lack of self-love. They can suppress the immune systems, and such immuno-suppression leads to infections and malignancies. Autoimmune diseases like rheumatoid arthritis, primary ovarian failure, adrenal atrophy and diabetes, and even coronary artery disease may also be indirectly attributed to *chakra* dysfunction.

Psycho-neuro-immunology researchers have found that patients suffering from severe depression, loneliness and grief suffered low activity of the thymus gland, and decreased T-lymphocytes (or T-cells that fight infections) and NK-cells (or natural killer cells that fight cancer) count.

Often, a blockage in one *chakra* affects another. For example, on account of sacral *chakra* blockage, frequent sexual contacts promote positive HIV status. Because of poor self-image associated with negative cultural views, an imbalance occurs in the heart *chakra* as well. This leads to thymic dysfunction and immuno-suppression, causing full expression of the disease. Modern science fails to recognize the importance of such *emotional immunity,* when it comes to the expression from "carrier state," to full-blown illness.

Throat Chakra

Symbolic of its position around the vocal cords, the throat *chakra* is essentially a communicative and creative center. It transfers energy to the thyroid, parathyroid gland and the larnyx. It is no wonder that the energies of many artists are concentrated here. Without the creative power to form words or vocalize a song, how could a writer or musician successfully write or sing?

The throat *chakra* is the center of *will.* Will encourages us to communicate with one another, and to verbally express new ideas. A musician will devote himself entirely to his song, not just for his own enjoyment, but for others as well. When jazz legend Miles Davis recorded *Sketches of Spain* in 1959, he completely absorbed the language and musical customs of the Spanish culture. His one distinction was that he played the trumpet, and not a Spanish flamenco guitar, to perform his *cante hondo,* or "deep song."

Inadequate energy flow to the throat *chakra* is most notable in over or underactivity of the thyroid gland, laryngitis and cancer of the lungs, larynx, throat and mouth. Lack of expression literally silences us, so that our negative emotions become bottled up inside. If they are never vented, or given a means of expression, they eventually manifest physically, and cause damage.

Brow Chakra

The "third eye of man," or the brow *chakra,* is represented by the energy polarity between the pituitary and the pineal glands.

This third eye in humans is the seat of intuition and clairvoyance. Meditation develops the third eye *chakra,* and intuitiveness. This inward focusing, or introspection results in clear insight and the power of discrimination. Because the center rests between the eyebrows, this *chakra* is the source of our intellect and wisdom. At this level is the habitat of our ears, eyes, nose and sinuses, as well as the origin of the spinal cord, pineal and pituitary gland.

Chakra dysfunction at this level can result in major endocrine imbalances. Recent scientific research in the field of Psycho-neuro-immunology has also revealed the deeper connections between the mind, endocrine and immune systems.

If the *chakras* in the fetal body do not provide the necessary sustaining energies to the developing organs, there is malfunctioning at the cellular, physical level. The *chakras* are the energy repositories of *karma,* and are bound by the law of cause and effect. For example, a severe blockage in the heart center—relating to an inability to express love or compassion, or "hard-heartedness" in a

Chakra Location	Nerve Plexus	Endocrine Gland	Psychological Correlate	Physiological Correlate
ROOT	Sacral	Gonads	Grounding	Reproduction
SACRAL	Hypogastric	Leydig	Sexuality	Excretion
NAVEL	Solar	Adrenal	Ego	Digestion
HEART	Cardiac	Thymus	Love	Circulation
THROAT	Cervical	Thyroid	Will	Respiration
BROW	Hypothalamus	Pituitary	Intuition	Autonomic
CROWN	Cerebral Cortex	Pineal	Spiritual	Higher Function

past life—might manifest itself as a congenital heart defect in a newborn baby.

The cosmic law of *karma* operates on the metaphysical level and states that every *action* produces an equal and opposite *reaction*. So *karmic* illnesses appearing as developmental abnormalities in an infant—or those that occur later on in life—are believed to be reactions to what had happened in previous lifetimes. Modern medicine fails to acknowledge this because it refers to the physical body as locked within a *linear* time frame, rather than *cyclical*.

It is not only the past carry-overs that affect the *chakras*, but also our present reaction to the environment. We may not be able to totally change what has already occurred, but we can certainly influence our future.

"So do our actions, and frame of mind determine our illness or wellness?" Bryan asks.

The power of positive thinking or affirmation is underestimated by modern medicine, even though it negates the *karmic* afflictions and enhances the *chakra* function. An illness relating to a past life is an unseen connection; therefore it is often difficult to perceive. Only through true comprehension of the subtle anatomy can the meaning of disease be understood.

More and more doctors are realizing how important the mind-body-soul connection is, and are discovering that meditation is a powerful tool that individuals can wield to prevent, master, or entirely conquer their disease. Each lifetime is an opportunity to evolve our *awareness* to higher levels.

Obstacles in the way of a meditative lifestyle are quite frequently the by-products of our own thinking and mental conditioning. Negative thought processes manifest as illness in our physical bodies. Depending on the specific impediment, disease appears in the organ closest to the impaired *chakra*.

Thirty to seventy percent of all drug and surgical intervention is merely a placebo effect, working more on the mind than on the body. Our immune system is highly thought-sensitive. Image and belief in a patient's mind that a substance can heal is often enough to counteract illness. On the other hand, negative thoughts can be *mental poisons*, and produce adverse effects: giving a patient only a certain amount of time to live can severely affect survival.

The fear of death, that hidden, constant fear that no amount of money or power can neutralize, is at the core of most negativity. If people only understood that *awareness* is a continuum, then this fear would dissolve.

Previously, Dr. Weiss was skeptical about life after death and distrusted anything that he thought could not be proven by traditional scientific methods. Because of his success with Catherine, his own life took on new meaning.

She had recorded that her experience of death was the same every time. Around the moment of death, her consciousness would depart from, and float above her body. She was then drawn to a warm and energizing light.

Inspired by her revelation, Dr. Weiss began to meditate, which was something, he thought, only Hindus and Californians practiced.

As told to Dr. Weiss by Catherine: "Energy, everything is energy . . . to be in a physical state is abnormal. When you are in spiritual state, that is natural to you."

The wheels of energy continue to turn, and the creative forces of the universe take us along, making us a part of all that there is.

Chapter Ten

Window to Awareness

To see a World in a grain of sand,
And a Heaven in a wild flower,
Hold Infinity in the palm of your hand,
And Eternity in an hour.
—William Blake

Ask someone in a meditative state, "Are you awake?" The answer will be "No." Ask them again, "Are you dreaming?" They will say "No." Ask that same person, "Are you asleep?" Their answer will still be "No."

We are probably wondering if this is some kind of cryptic riddle concocted by the yogis. If we are not awake, sleeping or dreaming, then where are we and what are we doing? Is it possible to enter a *fourth dimension*? Does it really exist?

Until now, we have recognized the two distinct states of consciousness as wakefulness, and sleep. And it is likely that we equate sleeping with dreaming. According to western philosophy, human beings are either actively going about their lives, or sleeping. It was the ancient yoga philosophers who insisted that wakefulness, sleeping and dreaming are three separate states. The fourth state, or *meditative dimension*, has nothing in common with the first three; it is not a state of doing, but of *being*.

When we are awake, asleep or dreaming, we depend on the environment in one way or another, as external objects and situations dictate our behavior. In meditation, however, our goal is to become aware of nothing other than our own *awareness*. In a meditative state, we are independent from the objects and situations around us, and are only aware.

From the moment we are born, we are conditioned to base our existence only on what we can directly perceive or experience through the immediate senses.

After a mother delivers, there is a sigh of relief when the baby is born with all its faculties intact, or with "ten fingers and ten toes." Doctors are especially concerned with how well the baby can see and hear. If the newborn gurgles with pleasure at the sounds of its parent's voices, and can recognize their faces, their ability to function is then confirmed.

"If a baby is born blind and deaf, are they then less aware?" Nicole asks.

Like blind bats that navigate the night with their acute ability to detect sound, handicapped babies must rely on their sense of touch and smell in order to recognize their parents. This, however, does not compromise their self-awareness. Regardless of his hearing impediment, Beethoven's musical genius expressed itself in his symphonies with a *sense* or *feel* for the music. Musicians like Stevie Wonder and Ray Charles are also not hindered by their blindness; they play great piano in spite of it.

In the embryonic stage, a fetus resides in a perfectly natural state. Amazingly, what the unborn fetus achieves involuntarily is what we human beings seek voluntarily in meditation. After all, a fetus' state is *being*. Even though the senses of sight, sound, smell, taste and touch are developing, the sensory stimulation is minimal. The self of the embryo experiences the pure Self. Curled into the fetal position, it is instinctively aware of *becoming* a human being. Likewise, the self of the meditating person sitting in the lotus position experiences the Self, and becomes aware of *just being*.

Meditation is an entirely non-verbal state of *awareness*; it is our inner world of individual experiences. I tell Nicole and Bryan that it earned its esoteric reputation because the experience itself is indescribable. A breathtaking sunset loses its shade of meaning when the experience is expressed in words. Like the plethora of colors that fill the sky, meditation is a state when our entire linguistic analysis is translated into inner experience.

Unlike *contemplation*, meditation has no use for thoughts. It utilizes both the left and right hemispheres of the brain, so that our respective logical and creative sides come to a quintessence.

When we are awake, the left side of the brain enable us to do things like *organize* lesson plans or *solve* a complicated computer technicality. With the right side of the brain, we are able to *imagine* a more *creative* lesson plan or solution. If it were not for the yogis in deep meditation who discovered the decimal and zero, mathematics, modern science, and computing would never have evolved. After all, it would be impossible to multiply in Roman numerals, i.e. XIII times XI = ?

Yogis combined logic with intuitiveness, for wisdom transcends both! In a meditative state, we transcend both the concrete and the abstract, and call only upon the quiet power of *awareness*.

Though it is a *no-mind state*, meditation is not an escape into a world of fiction, fantasy or imagination, nor is it any kind of tense concentration. Ironically, most people equate concentration with tension. True concentration, however, can only be achieved in a relaxed state. Meditation is the sound of silence, the evenness of breath and the release of muscle tension. Our resulting tranquility comes from touching the pure *awareness*, the core of our *being*.

Concentration in meditation, like controlling the breath or intoning a *mantra* syllabic formula—is not to be confused with either *hypnosis* or *trance*. Unlike meditation, there is an external influence involved in a hypnotic or trance-like state; a second party may be responsible for coercing, and enticing us, or putting us under a "spell." In the sense that we are forever following the suggestions of others, most of us are already hypnotized. Sometimes, the pressure of suggestion is so strong that we are not only moved against our will, but also become dependent on the person making them. In either state, there is suggestion, which means action taken. In meditation, we are observers, and not participants, for it is a *self-directed* observation.

Meditation is like watching a beautiful Arabian horse gallop across a field. By *observing* the long, graceful limbs of the animal and the freedom of its movements, we quietly celebrate the beauty of nature. By saddling the horse and riding away with it, we are *participating*, as in hypnosis. *Focusing* on the pleasure of the ride is like a trance.

Only when we change our perspective from *participation* to *observation*, can we begin to meditate. We then learn to witness *awareness* itself, and not simply its contents. This opens the gate of cosmic understanding. Enlightenment is achieved when the "observer" and the "observed" merge into one. When we acknowledge hidden levels of our *being*, we touch our inner wisdom and come to know "who we really are."

We achieve this "concentrated stillness," when we meditate. The great yoga master Patanjali, who authored the *Yoga Sutra*, defined meditation as "*the cessation of the agitation of consciousness.*" Like the rising and falling waves that surrender in the ocean, our thoughts in meditation are absorbed into the platitude of experience.

In yoga philosophy, *Dharana* is the capacity of the individual to focus the mind at will. It has long been known that Buddha meditated for a continuous vigil of forty-nine days and forty-nine nights. In the past twenty-six centuries, no one has ever broken such a record, perhaps because there is no Olympic competition in stillness!

Like Buddha, we can also transcend the very existence of our physical self. When we open our eyes and return from our meditative state, we may be surprised, for instance, at our spatial orientation, and the amount of time that had elapsed. We accomplish a heightened state of *awareness* when we finally become oblivious to objects or stimuli outside of ourselves.

The method of meditation is a private one. Though I have taught several of my patients to meditate, there is no action or judgment on my part. As a physician and a yoga practitioner, I can personally attest that meditation lessens the intensity of a host of ailments, and that *meditation is the best medication.* Ranging from hypertension, drug abuse, alcoholism, cancer, cardiac diseases and immune disorders, we can learn to heal what is broken in us.

Nicole inquires how meditation can help her overcome chronic stress and negativity.

If we consciously note the state of our everyday mind, we find it preoccupied with constant chatter. Every thought is an answer to the preceding thought—a never-ending continuum. In this inner dialogue we indulge in memories of the past, and worries of the future—forgetting to live in the "here and now." Such mind-chatter clouds our perceptions and interferes with the mind's clarity. But once we become *aware* of its negative tone, we develop the power to transform the unloving and self-condemning thoughts into positive and loving messages—converting *stress* into *strength.*

I will soon introduce Nicole and Bryan to those patients who have made such transformations. Seeking that *fourth dimension,* they accompany me into the "inner world" where the focused *awareness* interacts with the human physiology.

Chapter Eleven

Inner World

Namaste...I honor the place in you
in which the entire universe dwells.
I honor the place in you, which is
of love, of peace, of light and of truth.
When you are in that place in you,
and I am in that place in me...We are One.
—inspired by yoga literature

Inspired by my own revelation, I sought to answer why we feel "moved" by meditation and music, and what accounts for the physiological changes in our bodies. How does our physical self respond to transitions in our *awareness*? How do we explain this *inner experience*?

The *central processing unit* of our body's biocomputer is the brain and its extension, the spinal cord, which together constitute the *central nervous system*. Neuro-chemicals form the link between the brain—our *hardware*—and the mind—our *software*. The electrical *circuits* or nerves in the body belong to two powerful systems that transmit information and carry messages from the brain.

The first is the *voluntary* or *sensorimotor nervous system*, which controls both our senses and the muscles, thereby providing us with information about our inner sensations and outer environment. The other system is called the *involuntary* or *autonomic ner-*

vous system and regulates our internal organ systems, such as circulation and digestion.

The *autonomic nervous system* is a sophisticated energy network that maintains the balance and harmony in the body. It is called "autonomic" because it functions largely outside the bounds of conscious control. It is particularly involved with controlling our stress reactions and if we know how to "tame" this powerful system, we can free ourselves from stress and the diseases associated with it.

What we achieve through yoga is the ability to *act* in life, not *react*, for all reactions create imbalances in the *autonomic nervous system* and in what I call the "inner world."

Our "inner world" consists of the *limbic system*—the "seat of human emotion," the *pineal* and *pituitary glands*, and the *hypothalamus*. The small powerful brain "microchip" *hypothalamus* sits at the base of the brain, and governs both the *endocrine* and the *au-*

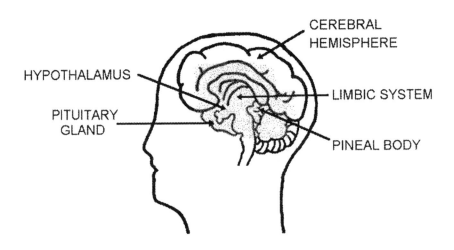

FIGURE 9. INNER WORLD

tonomic nervous system. It is the brain's brain and mind's gateway to health. Interestingly enough our "inner world," corresponds to the *ajna,* or *brow chakra*—the central focus of meditation. (Fig.9) The two limbs of the autonomic system—*sympathetic* and *para-sympathetic*—work to keep the bodily organs under a dual control. They are not complete polar opposites, but are actually *comple-mentary.* Like our right and left-hand work together, a dynamic equilibrium exists between the two limbs when we are healthy. Both systems innervate the heart, for example. In normal circum-stance, a balance between the two limbs determines the resting heart rate—about 70 beats per minute. *Sympathetic* stimulation speeds up the heart rate and creates arousal in the body; while the *parasympathetic* slows the heart beat and induces inhibition or rest in the body.

In the event of a threat, our *sympathetic system* provides the alarm or arousal for defense—the familiar "flight or fight response." When we are startled, feel under attack or encounter everyday stress, our whole body reacts with muscle tension. On the other hand, the *parasympathetic* for the most part generates an inhibitory response and is site-specific, like slowing of the heart beat. A fainting spell from fear of pain or actual pain, in the dentist chair indicates slow-ing of the heartbeat due to *parasympathetic* predominance even in the face of overall arousal. We never utilize *only* one half of our *autonomic nervous system.*

Both limbs are stimulated by environmental stress however, and it is our individual reaction to the perceived threat that determines the neurological balance. The two systems are built, and function, differently. The *sympathetic* coordinates an overall "global" response, while the *parasympathetic* is "focal" or site-specific; therefore we have almost infinite combinations between arousal and inhibition.

Characterized by excessive dominance of either arousal or inhibi-tion, stress is a state of autonomic imbalance. *Acute* stress is usu-ally thought of as just a "flight or fight response," culminating in a rise of blood pressure, heart rate, breathing and increase in muscle tension.

We become aroused by a threat, and even when the threat disappears, it leaves a subtle, *residual alertness* in our subconscious. When we *think* there is danger—even if there is none—we react like there is. Our thoughts and perceptions determine the intensity of this alarm reaction.

For instance, a workaholic—because of *time urgency*—has such a reaction. His or her small day to day worries become large issues, and this *chronic* stress prevents complete relaxation.

If such stress continues, or if, in addition, new threats arise, our body begins to deplete its resources, leading to "burnout," easy fatigue and exhaustion. Remaining in such a state of *constant arousal*—without seeking relief—sets the stage for physiological breakdown: illness, disease and premature death.

Strangely enough, *parasympathetic*-related stress has received very little attention, although two common ailments—ulcer and asthma— are manifestations of increased *vagus nerve* activity, the major component of the *parasympathetic system*. The reaction to the threat becomes not confrontation, but withdrawal. In what is termed the "possum" reaction, it manifests physiologically by decreased heart rate, blood pressure and breathing, and increased lethargy.

A sense of *helplessness* and *hopelessness* turns the body's systems in low gear, so the person becomes depressed and unmotivated. Inactivity sets in, like it does for a "couch potato." Losing the capacity to function results in chronic fatigue, and severe depression may contribute to the onset of cancer.

Long-term practitioners of yoga and meditation develop great control over the *autonomic nervous system*. Yogis like Swami Rama and others have demonstrated to Western scientists their ability to selectively regulate their heartbeats, lower their blood pressure and affect the temperature of their skin. In one experiment by Elmer E. Green, at the Menninger Foundation, Swami Rama voluntarily induced a run of *atrial flutter*—a rapid and irregular heart beat of 300 beats per minute—for 17 seconds! He also was able to enter a state of deep sleep while remaining conscious, as evidenced by a slight gentle snore and a steady stream of *delta* brain waves.

Meditation helps to restore the balance in the *autonomic nervous system*, infusing us with inner strength to withstand the environmental stress.

The infamous "silent killers"—hypertension and high cholesterol—often have no warning symptoms and yet are implicated in heart attacks and strokes. In 1974, a study conducted at Harvard Medical School established the lowering of blood pressure by meditation and similar results were subsequently reported in many other studies.

During their research in Israel, Angia Cooper and Emmin Aygen found that meditation also lowered abnormally high cholesterol levels. Incorporating these ideas, Dr. Dean Ornish's much-publicized program—which includes meditation—has shown the reversal of coronary artery disease: the leading cause of death in the United States.

Asthmatic patients practicing yoga and meditative techniques have demonstrated fewer asthma attacks, less need for medication and greater control over their breathing. A study done on 2000 meditators by Dr. David Johnson revealed that meditators saw their doctor only half as often as the average American and had significantly less number of hospital admissions.

To understand how the body reacts during a meditative state, Dr. Itzhak Bentov, a long-term meditator himself, conducted a study of repetitive meditation over time. Using an instrument called a ballistocardiograph; he measured bodily changes that occur in heart and brain activity during deep states of meditation in his subjects. He found that during meditation, a unique biofeedback system between the heart and aorta produced micro-oscillations in the body, which in turn stimulated certain pathways of the brain.

In a meditative state, our breathing becomes extremely slow, and activity in the heart is so synchronized that it creates a resonant vibrational link between the heart and the brain. According to Bentov, a circulating current in the sensory motor cortex of the brain is gradually established when we continue to meditate over time. This in turn *releases* old stresses locked into the brain tissue itself. The establishment of *new* neural pathways prevents stress from reaccumulating, and actually stimulates the pleasure centers instead.

Besides being responsible for changes in the neural pathways, meditation helps restore *chakra* function, reducing the potential for disease and decreasing the intensity of any pre-existing illness.

The major *chakras* transform energy flow from the *nadis* and distribute it to the major endocrine glands, nerve plexuses and organs of the body. The *negatively entropic* fluid –like energies flowing through the *nadis* become converted into a neuro-hormonal signal. Since *chakra dysfunction* occurs on account of acquired and/or "carried-over" *karmic* energies, meditation—by mending the "broken wheels"—provides emotional and physical immunity.

Long-term meditators demonstrate far greater coherence of brain wave activity between the right and left *cerebral hemispheres* than those who do not meditate. Aligning our nervous system balances our *milieu-interior,* or internal chemistry.

The two complementary aspects of *awareness* are expressed through the right and left *cerebral hemispheres*. In a right-handed person, the left brain is the "linear thinking mind," representing our more analytical, mathematical, verbal selves, and the right brain in turn constitutes the "emotional intelligence," expressing our

82

artistic, esthetic, intuitive and spatial qualities. In a left-handed person, it is just the opposite.

Nicole admits being more "right-sided," since she is both creatively and emotionally inclined, and relates to words and concepts rather than numbers or formulae. Bryan counters that he relates to not abstract entities, but to logic and reason instead.

But imagine having *both* sides working full-time, contributing 100% of their effort! Empirically speaking, the average human being only utilizes a mere 15% of their daily brainpower. To increase the per-centile of brain activity, the two halves of the brain need to be synchronized. In most of us—like Nicole and Bryan—they are lat-eralized, so we become fragmented in our thinking.

Greater synchronization between the right and left hemispheres as seen in long-term meditators has been associated with greater cre-ativity and flexibility of thought. The whole process of meditation is about stilling the mind and relinquishing the thought process.

Thoughts are *energy forms* and arise from the *samskaras*, or sub-liminal impressions stored in the unconscious. These are deeply embedded memories in the *subtle body* and are carried forth through countless life cycles. We are strongly influenced by these *data banks* formatted in our previous and present lives. Consequently, our belief systems—or what we are conditioned to believe—is what we ultimately manifest and experience.

As powerful as these thoughts are to us, they are just as influen-tial on others. And though it is often hard to comprehend, what *one individual* thinks ultimately affects the *entire world*. This phe-nomenon is demonstrated in the *Maharishi Effect*, or the rise of the collective *awareness* in any community. In 1974, American social scientists discovered that when only one percent of a town's popu-lation practiced meditation, the overall crime rate decreased, indi-cating increasing order and harmony.

The same effect was witnessed on a global scale. In 1988, three large "World Peace Assemblies" were held over a period of two to three weeks in the United States, Holland and India. The two superpowers of the time—the United States and the Soviet Union—coincidentally, ended their long-standing enmity with a friendly handshake.

Bryan relates these phenomena to holographic interconnectedness, and that one part affects the whole.

Thoughts even in the subtlest dimensions manipulate electromagnetic fields and affect one's perception. As energy waves, they vibrate and the *frequency* of reverberation and the distance in *polarity* creates stress and tension. The more accelerated the *frequency* and wider the distance in *polarity*, the greater the stress.

If we think *dual* or discriminatory thoughts, our actions in life will usually parallel that. But if we think *non-dual*, unified and elevated thoughts, our contributions to human evolution are of a positive nature.

Dual thoughts are limiting, as they dwell on the "pair of opposites," such as "yours" and "mine," "us" and "them." Inherently contained in dual thoughts are wider *polarity*, or separateness, and accelerated *frequency* of vibration. Therefore, dual thoughts create greater tension and stress, and lead to limited and *contracted awareness*. It is no wonder then that an average person is essentially 85% dead to life!

Meditative thinking is more *non-dual* in nature, celebrating *unity in diversity*. Due to minimal distance in *polarity* and slow *frequency*, *non-dual* thought creates minimal stress. As the thought forms of meditators evolve from the *dual* to the *non-dual*, there is progression from incoherence to coherence, and hence *expanded awareness*. They develop a sense of "one equality consciousness," in which every living thing on the planet shares. They become conscious that the Self and the universe both stem from a single source. Superficial differences between people, like racial and ethnic background or religious preference, become irrelevant non-issues.

When our thoughts are less fragmented, our thinking mind is free to utilize its higher functioning powers. Such synchronization becomes evident when our brain waves are recorded as deep and slow, as *delta* waves. This leads us to a better understanding of the four brain waves: *beta, alpha, theta* and *delta.*

As we progress from *beta* to *delta waves,* the amplitude increases and the frequency decreases. This corresponds with increasing synchrony of the brain's two hemispheres. The brain is most lateralized when the high frequency *beta* waves are predominant. (16 cycles per second). As the brain waves slow down, hemispheric synchrony dawns in the *alpha,* (10 cycles per second) and deepens in the *theta* (8 cycles per second). Total synchronization is augmented in the dominant *delta* frequency, (4 cycles per second) as it occurs exclusively during deep sleep and meditation.

Deep sleep and meditation are such synchronous states that they bring forth secretions of natural opiates, or endorphins within the brain. This validates the blissful, euphoric state of *awareness* in deep meditation and relaxation in restful sleep.

The vehicle of music induces synchronization and expands our *awareness* as well. From everyday fixed time and space it opens wider vistas of timeless, boundless reality. The melodic vibrations bring about *resonance* in the "inner world" with psycho-physiological consequences. By affecting our "stream of sensitivity," such reverberation transports us from our objective to subjective consciousness, and then to the subconscious quantum reality. Sound energy acts as a "microwave" and influences the oscillating quantum fields. It was then this internal rhythm that transcended me to a world of *timeless awareness.* Touching the fringes of infinity, the music, and I, the musician had merged into one.

Only when we tune out the external world and its surroundings are we completely focused on and responsive to our "inner world"— that part of us which is constantly refined by meditation, or music.

Meditation is no miracle cure for stress, yet patients who meditate consistently become better equipped to handle stress in the environment. Since human beings are mentally able to *reflect* on a situation *before* reacting, how we *perceive* a stressful situation will determine how we are *affected* by it.

When someone angers us, our first reaction is usually to retaliate. If we stop to take a deep breath however, we give ourselves time to think, and to realize that our own reaction may only escalate a situation. Meditation teaches us that not every situation necessarily has to warrant a reaction from us. Acting as a kind of "shock absorber" for stress, it grants us more *tolerance* and develops the foundation to face the adversities of life.

Meticulous organization and design is involved when an architect begins to construct a building. To achieve perfection, every intricate detail must be attended to. Throwing a few bricks and stones together will never yield a breathtaking cathedral. The delicate iconography is just as important as the underlying structure. Responsible for a cathedral that lasts for a thousand years is this solid architecture and careful planning.

Building a *less-imperfect* mind employs the same attention. Man is the architect of his own destiny, and he can choose to either build his world on a flimsy foundation, or one on solid ground. Likewise, our minds can either wander unfocused, or direct our attention to the horizon of *unobstructed awareness*.

Meditation can help us design our own quality blueprints, so that they are beautifully sketched across the vast canvas of life. Once the blemishes are removed, we are able to *remain* focused, and dwell in the eternal richness somewhere within us.

Chapter Twelve

Discovering Self

More minute than the minute,
More expansive than the most expansive
Space of the whole universe,
This Self of the Being is hidden in a cave.
—Katha Upanishad

Four months ago today, Nicole and Bryan paid their first visit to my office. On that crisp evening in October, when the leaves were just beginning to turn from green to gold, Nicole told me that she was seeking relief from her ever-present anxiety *without* medication. As a teacher, she was an open-minded recipient of all this ancient wisdom, ready from the beginning to learn new ways of looking at life, though Bryan was mostly along for the ride. Because of his technical, mechanical way of looking at the world, he often saw no room for philosophical thinking in his life.

The November rains and December holidays passed, and I continued to guide Nicole along the path of holistic healing. While providing Bryan with scientific evidence for each step of our journey, something quite extraordinary happened.

He had been highly skeptical and even cynical about the philosophy of meditation, but told me that he had seen his doctor before the New Year and his cholesterol had risen substantially since his last annual checkup. He confessed that what supported the thousand year-old pillars of yoga and meditation was worth pursuing.

"I now look at holistic medicine with a new perspective," Bryan confides.

To a physician like myself, who once regarded "complementary" medicine as less effective than "conventional" methods, have come to believe that meditation has truly enhanced my life, and the lives of my patients.

It is February, 14 days away from Nicole and Bryan's wedding. All of the preparations for the ceremony have long been finalized, leaving them a little more time to incorporate meditation into their lifestyle. They, along with my four other patients, will finally get to participate in the actual process of meditating. All six meditators will reap the same benefits: a clearer, calmer mind, a balanced, more coordinated body and an *awareness* of the universal energy. Each of them will learn to ascend into their own inner worlds, and communicate with the healing centers that reside therein.

We gather in my office on this late-afternoon winter day. The sun casts a pure light on the blanket of snow outside as I introduce my four patients to Nicole and Bryan. Even though we are all at differ-ent meditative levels—I have made it an integral part of my lifestyle, some of my patients have recently adopted it, and Nicole and Bryan are just about to embrace it. Meditation is an ongoing learning process, and a constant uncovering of the hidden, inner mysteries of the higher Self.

Joe, 55, a branch manager at a local bank in the process of merg-ing with another bank, underwent triple bypass surgery after he was diagnosed with coronary heart disease three years ago. Be-tween an impending merger and heart disease, Joe's lack of cer-tainty about the future—a distinctly human source of *stress*—Joe was under acute stress. When he eventually lost his job after the bank was bought out, he was forced to work much longer hours at a smaller bank for less income. He smoked heavily, and required balloon angioplasty for recurrent chest pains on two occasions, until he finally gave up smoking after his second intervention. When he came to see me, he was being maintained on several heart medications. We started meditation therapy, but kept him on the medication.

"That was a year ago, and since then, I have not needed any medication for chest pains," he says. "Meditation weaned me off most of my medication. It seems like once my health got better; my whole outlook on life did, too. I became partners with a man I worked with—who had come into some money—and we started our own mortgage service company."

Nicole relates to Joe of a man she read about in a health magazine whose heart problems were also resolved by meditation. It was that one article that inspired her to come to me for her own stress and anxieties.

With his entrepreneurial venture becoming a slow but steady success, Joe now makes the time to pursue old hobbies, like his golf game. He never realized before how much he disliked compromising himself for the success of others, until he began to meditate.

Stress is also nothing new to Mike, 50. For the past fifteen years, he had climbed the corporate ladder at a feverish pace. The rush to succeed induced a sense of *time urgency*, and introduced a certain *hostility* to his previously friendly nature. Too little time at home had caused problems in his marriage, and he turned to alcohol for solace. Too many "power lunches" and not enough exercise put 35 extra pounds on, and he developed moderately severe high blood pressure. Vying for the Vice-Presidency at his insurance company, he also compromised his health for success. A previous doctor put him on medication for hypertension, but he needed stress reduction as well.

In the past 6 months since he has been my patient, he has lost eighteen pounds, eliminated his alcohol intake, makes healthy food choices and most importantly, works decent hours since he has overcome his *time urgency* and *hostility*. He has been meditating regularly, and his marriage situation has improved.

"I even showed my wife how to meditate, and I took off last month so we could spend some time at Hilton Head," Mike tells us. "If you told me last year that I would be opting for a silent retreat at the shore instead of at the office, I would've said you were crazy!"

Mike's rising blood pressure has plateaued; it does not fluctuate like it used to, but remains effectively controlled by the same amount of medication.

"I have really been making an effort to fit meditation into my schedule, so I do it every morning before I go to work," Mike says. "I swear, it changes my whole day because I'm more calm and collected, and I don't fly off the handle anymore when a deal falls through."

Erin, a homemaker in her mid-forties, has suffered periods of *insomnia*. Last year, she underwent lumpectomy followed by a series of radiation treatments for breast cancer. Even though Erin had been physically in remission, she was preoccupied by the constant *fear* that it would reoccur, or manifest itself in another part of her body. She was so afraid of becoming sick again that she became a "cancer cripple"—she would visit her doctor almost every week with imagined "symptoms," and when her tests continued to come back as negative, she would seek other doctors for a second opinion.

It was Erin's sister who had been my patient once, and after spending night after night on the phone with Erin—who had stopped sleeping, and stayed up to read article after article on cancer survivors—she referred her to me.

"You see, my mother died a very painful death from breast cancer, since it was too late to stop the disease once they found the malignancy," she confides. "She was the same age as I am now, and I never want to suffer like she did. I was preoccupied with the cancer, and afraid that it was waiting to strike again."

Meditation is an antidote to *fear*, *anxiety*, and *depression* because it was able to carry Erin's disturbed mind to its own inner sanctuary—the "retreat" and place of refuge inside us that is free from any sensory or emotional upheaval. Since she has started to meditate, she has overcome most of her self-condemnation and conversion reaction.

"For so long, I could not play my piano, and music has always been such a comfort to me," Erin says. "There was just no joy in me for so long, and now that I've resumed, I feel like myself, only much more aware."

Both meditation and music transport us from the adversity of life to the magical world of heightened *awareness*. These are the means we can call upon to create order from chaos, and harmony from noise.

Not only does meditation have a bolstering effect on heart disease, hypertension and cancer; it also can positively alter a patient's immune system. When patients learn they are HIV-positive, their mental outlook may influence whether or not they develop the AIDS virus. Immune disorders like AIDS physically weaken a person so that they become extremely vulnerable to any kind of infection and cancer, and a *negative mentality* can actually precipitate deterioration.

Andre, 26, was referred to me by a psychiatrist friend. Eight months ago, Andre's blood test came back HIV-positive. For almost three years, he had been addicted to heroin, using the drug intravenously. As is the habit of those in the clutches of addiction, Andre shared his syringes with fellow users.

"All you know is the drug, and you need to shoot so bad that you don't even think about the needles being contaminated," he says. "That's how I got AIDS."

Andre has not developed any of the symptoms that characterize AIDS yet, and his CD 4-cell count remains normal. His bodily immunity seems to be holding, and I believe that it is because he has made such significant changes in his lifestyle. He is continuing drug rehabilitation and psychiatric counseling, and he is also learning to meditate, which helps him control his urge for the heroin.

Emotional immunity to disease is often underestimated and overlooked by mainstream medicine. Meditation is a powerful tamer of unchecked desires, and substance abuse is nothing more than the desire to *escape* the pain of day-to-day reality through artificial means. Injecting drugs is a dangerous detour, and such a lifestyle is synonymous with risk, as Andre discovered when he contracted HIV. The "natural high" achieved in meditation is like a pure substitute for the "artificial high" that heroin provides, and is far more effective in the long run. More importantly, Andre has remained asymptomatic, and hopefully will continue to be less of a risk to himself.

"Something about meditation keeps me coming back for more," he confides to the group. "Every time I did rehab, I'd end up back on the streets sooner or later. But this gives me some kind of new connection to the world, so I don't need to fall back on that drug like I used to. I am more in touch with myself now, so I started writing poetry again."

The teachings of ancient wisdom—of which my six modern thinkers have so recently become enlightened—will continuously be applied from here on.

Though it originated five thousand years ago, yoga is now considered part of the "new age" movement. Even to the learned, yoga is still shrouded in dark mysteries and is an unattainable art for the average person. Those who are unfamiliar with yoga and meditation often make the misconception that it is a strange and foreign *religion*, even a cult. They might falsely assume that those who meditate are only of a certain origin or country, or that they all shave their heads and wear orange, flowing robes.

Yoga is *not* a secret sect to which a select few can belong. There is no "black magic" in yoga, nor is it mandatory to wear a costume or uniform in order to meditate. The art of yoga was discovered long before any religion in the entire world was organized—two thousand years ago. In fact, most religions have unknowingly incorporated several tenets of yoga philosophy in their doctrines.

Yoga is a philosophy, a practical science and a discipline that *any one*—student, teacher, homemaker, artist, doctor, businessman, technician, manual laborer—can make a part of their day-to-day life.

At the heart of yoga is spiritual *awareness*. And although spirituality is the core of all of the world's major religions, most organized practices operate as dual entities—separate and competitive. Fundamentalist religious leaders and their followers continuously compete for dominance. After all, more human beings have died in religious wars than in any others.

Polarity

For daily meditation, it is important to choose a *place*, which will be used regularly for practice. Continually coming back to the same room or other space, is a way to "mark" our spiritual territory. In the space where we sit, we create vibrational energy that contains our individual essence, so the surrounding atmosphere remains our own. Wherever we decide to sit and meditate should be somewhere comfortable, free from clutter, noise, pollution and the distractions of other people. Comfort is essential, because we will be sitting for an extended amount of time. Most meditators prefer to sit on a soft mat, or carpeted surface, which provides comfort as well as *insulation* from the Earth's magnetic field.

When we sit, we should position our body to face *North* or *East*. The element iron found in our bodies is responsible for magnetically aligning us with the Earth's polarity. In each cubic millimeter of blood, we have 5 million red blood cells circulating and each cell contains an iron molecule. This *ferrous magnetism* in our physiology parallels itself to the Earth's magnetic fields, so we are naturally "pulled" in the right directions. If our body is physically aligned during meditation, we become the ideal recipients of the higher forces at play in a balanced mind.

The *temperature* of the room is also important. If we are drowsy from the heat, or shivering with the cold, we will be unable to concentrate during meditation. Striking a balance between a high and low temperature is the ideal. It is a good idea to have some fresh air circulating in the room by leaving the window just open a bit, since our mind must be alert during meditation. Since the body's metabolism tends to slow down when we meditate, placing a light blanket or shawl over the shoulders for extra warmth will do.

Appointment

When we designate a fixed time to practice, our mind and body become more accustomed to the process of meditation. It is best to be consistent, and meditate at a certain time. The ideal times to meditate are sunrise, 6:00 a.m., 12:00 noon, sunset, or 6:00 p.m. At these times, the gravitational pull of the sun works in harmony with the natural polarity in our body.

According to the yogis, the most auspicious and peaceful time to engage in meditation is between the early hours of 4:00 a.m. and 6:00 a.m. They called this time the *brahmamuhurta*, or "hour of the Lord," since there seems to be a strange and mystical aura about these hours. The stillness and ambiance in the atmosphere is particularly conducive for meditating. It is at this time that most births and deaths occur across the planet. Our *awareness* is also transiting from sleep to wakefulness, like the rising sun unveils the curtain of darkness.

Within the span of these transitional hours, the breath flows equally and readily through both nostrils, and the *sushumna nadi* is relatively open—making it an ideal time for *transcendence.* Most people, however, pass these auspicious hours of the morning in sleep.

For the late-risers, early meditation can be a struggle. Some of us may not be morning people, and might opt to meditate in the evening around sunset instead. There are a few techniques I have developed over the years that have helped me establish a regular morning routine of meditation.

Most of us make many appointments with other people and places throughout the day, so why not reserve the *first appointment* for ourselves? After all, it is probably our most private—and possibly our only—time alone when we are left undisturbed and unburdened by other responsibilities. An ideal moment to nourish our mind, body and soul.

But what often makes it difficult to commit to such an early appointment is what we did the night before. Alcohol intake causes inertia in the body and leaves us feeling heavy and dull the next morning—hence the term "hangover." On the other hand, culprits like coffee, tea, colas and chocolate cause disturbed sleep because they overstimulate us. Either way, we wake up feeling unrefreshed and irritable, unable to concentrate.

Eating anything two hours—especially spicy foods—before retiring should also be avoided. Watching TV or reading the paper before bedtime effects the quality of our morning meditation, because what we watch or read leaves an aftertaste in our subconscious.

Quality sleep equals quality meditation, and that means getting to bed at a decent hour. On average, we need about 6 hours of restful sleep a night. Ideally, getting to bed by 10:00 p.m. gives us enough sleep. It is not the *quantity* of sleep that is important, but the *quality*. The deep sleep cycle usually occurs *before* 4:00 or 5:00 a.m., so any sleep after that is dream—and significantly less restful—sleep. As we progress in meditation, we might find that we are able to reduce the number of hours we need to sleep.

Duration

A novice might sit and meditate for only five or ten minutes. But it is more important to develop the *habit* of meditating regularly for a short time than to sit for an hour daydreaming, fantasizing or feeling bored.

Consistency of meditation is more relevant than the duration. With practice, we will remain centered in a meditative state for this period of time, until we can gradually lengthen the duration. Twenty minutes might be increased to an hour or more, depending on the depth of our meditations and our individual abilities and lifestyles.

The optimum amount of time for meditation is twenty-four minutes, because for every one minute the benefit lasts for an hour. Since meditation has no cumulative effect, it has to be practiced on a daily basis. But I know for certain that the more we meditate, the more we will want to meditate.

Once we choose a designated time, place and duration of meditation, we can personalize our "sanctuary" with whatever helps us to reach a heightened state. For those who have been meditating for awhile, spiritual accessories become non-essential. A novice, however, may utilize them for focus or ambiance.

Meditation is always an intimate experience, and it is up to the individual to decide what will or will not fill their sacred space. Any sensory accommodations we make serves to quieten our "inner world"—the very seat of our urges, emotions and desires.

Imagery

Focusing one or more of our senses helps us to overcome our thoughts. Candle gazing directs our thoughts by *visualization*, and it is often a prelude to deeper meditation. Ideally, meditating in a relatively dark area on the image of the flame provides us with just enough focus to transport our mind from the outer realm to the "inner world." The light of a candle guides us to the "light within"— a baseless and a smokeless flame.

Invocation

Sound produces mind-body-soul attunement. Listening to soothing, comforting and meditative music "sets the stage," putting us in the right frame of mind. For example, emotional evocations like Gregorian chants or any sacred music can induce what is known as "limbic kindling." When our "inner world" is continuously exposed to such sonic stimulus, the cells become more sensitive and attuned.

Being a musician, I often select Beethoven's *Piano Concerto No. 5*, " *Emperor*," Mozart's *Laudate Dominium*, Zamfir's romantic pan flute or an early morning Raga like *Bharav*.

A special syllabic arrangement, *mantra* helps us further immerse ourselves in our practice. This *mantra* is not selected for its meaning, but for its vibration. According to the quantum-physicist S.G. Hagelin, the syllables are actual sounds generated by the cosmic, unified field. Such reverberation entrains, or captures the internal rhythm, and leads us effortlessly to subtler levels of *awareness*. This intoning effects every part of our body and mind, right down to each cell and molecule. *Mantra* can therapeutically stimulate the cells, tissues, nerve plexus and organs by resonance.

In fact, specific *mantras* can stimulate specific *chakras*, thereby creating balance, and helps overcome existing dysfunction. Dr.

Motoyama confirms that *mantras* and *chakras* are intimately connected to the *nadis*, and an increase in the energy flow along these channels exerts a healing effect at all levels.

Representing the *ajna*, or *brow chakra*, the universal *mantra Om* is most often invoked in meditation. Called the "third eye," this center is the most transcendental, and is the realm of wisdom and universal intelligence. In linguistics, *O* is the synthesis of *A* and *U* and thus, it is verbalized as *Aum*. *A* is the first, and *M* is the last syllable in Sanskrit language. Representing the three states of *awareness*—awake, dream and sleep—*AUM* is believed to be the spoken essence of the universe and is intoned within. For those like Nicole, who are more emotionally inclined, may prefer to focus on *Yam*, the *mantra* for the *anahata chakra*, or heart center.

Aroma

Anointing the *chakras* with *aromatic oils* can be therapeutic, and evoke certain responses in our minds. The scent and touch of a particular oil can have a purifying effect on us. Patchouli, in particular, has antiseptic and anti-inflammatory benefits. Lavender and rose are calming, as jasmine and sandalwood help improve concentration.

Burning *incense* also induces and pervades the meditative atmosphere, creating an ethereal, contemplative aura.

Purity

Before we actually sit and meditate, it is important to cleanse the body both externally and internally. It is advisable to meditate on an empty stomach, or to wait at least four hours after a meal, so our body is not preoccupied with digesting food. Purifying the physical self helps to clear our mind of body consciousness. In turn, meditation cleanses the mental self for it is really *soap for the mind*!

Habitus

Essential to meditation is a steady, correct posture. The head, neck and spine *must* remain straight, but relaxed throughout. In this way, the *kundalini* energy can ascend through each *chakra*. If we slump forward, rounding the shoulders and malaligning the spine, we disrupt this ascension of *awareness*.

The traditional, or advanced posture is the *lotus* (Fig.10): the legs are crossed, and the right foot is placed on the left thigh, the left foot on the right. Beginners often adopt the *easy pose*, or a basic cross-legged position, because it is easier to achieve total muscle relaxation in this posture.

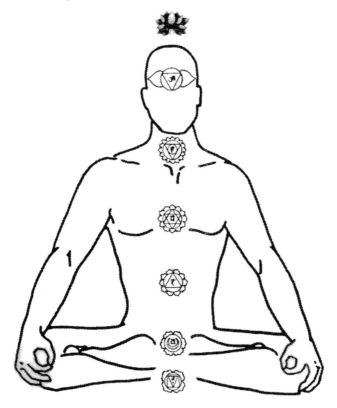

FIGURE 10. LOTUS POSTURE

For some people, especially those suffering from sciatica, sacral discomfort, or torn and injured cartilage in the knees, sitting cross-legged on the floor is too painful. Since there is never a *"no pain, no gain"* attitude in yoga, we must modify accordingly. Yoga should challenge our bodies, but not harm them, so meditation can *also* be practiced while remaining seated in an upright, armless chair. Sitting upright in the chair—ideally with our backs *away* from the back of the chair—our feet should be flat on the floor, about hip width apart. (Fig. 11)

Hands are placed on the knees, with the palms facing upwards. They can also be formed in a *mudra*, with the thumb and the fore-finger touching to make a circle, symbolizing the union between the individual and the universal Self.

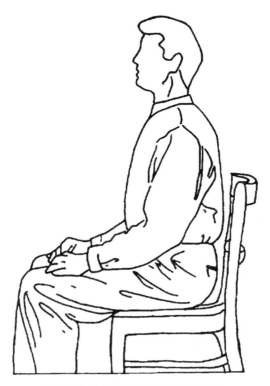

FIGURE 11. MEDITATIVE POSTURE

Cascade

In meditation, we should be as unrestricted as possible, so we wear loose, comfortable clothing, remove glasses or contact lenses and take off our shoes. Gently closing our eyes so we *withdraw* from all spaces and places, we take slow, deep and even breaths. Our breath should cascade like soft water through our lungs, without interruption or hesitation. Each of us will find a regular rate and rhythm of breathing within our own individual capacity.

When the breath is steady, the activity of the mind also becomes centered and focused. When we are able to maintain our attention directly on our breath, we become *aware* of a calm center within us.

It is more important to customize *one* method and routine, and master that completely, than to become a collector of many different techniques. Meditation can then become confusing, and overly complicated, and that is exactly what we are trying to avoid when we meditate!

Tides

In its natural state, an ocean is a bed of calm. Only with the rise and fall of the waves does it become rumpled or turbulent, and once the storm passes and the undercurrents subside, the waves quietly merge back into the ocean.

Like the waves in the ocean, our thoughts create turbulence in our mind. To transcend thoughts, we need to become independent of them. When a thought arises in meditation, rather, we *allow* it to *surface* and eventually settle back into the mind. We make no effort to fight or control it, because to battle with a thought is to become involved. Letting thoughts take precedence over meditation, we easily become carried away, and our *awareness* is compromised in the process. Wandering thoughts, fantasies and daydreams divert our attention away from the object of meditation—

ourselves—and into the external world.

Once the mind surrenders, and is no longer caught up in thought, we begin to witness *awareness*. What is commonly termed TM, or transcendental meditation, is really just meditation, for there is *no* meditation without transcendence!

Nicole and Bryan were married on Valentine's Day, a holiday that depicts the heart, and its infinite capacity for unconditional love. As Nicole walked down the aisle toward Bryan, I perceived the bride as *Shakti*, waiting to join her beloved groom *Shiva* at the altar. It is reminiscent of the marriage between the feminine *kundalini* energy and the masculine *sahasara* energy.

The rings have now been exchanged, the same ones that were so blurred in Nicole's mind at one time. Learning to convert stress into strength, she is no longer the overly anxious young woman who rushed into my office in October. Becoming more aware, Bryan himself is not as skeptical a thinker. As I have continued to guide them along in their journey, my fondness has grown. We have developed a mutual respect and rapport, quite like I do with every patient.

When we remain continually devoted to our practice no matter the level of experience, we maintain a serene and tranquil mind in the midst of earthly turmoil.

Legendary in yoga philosophy is the analogous lotus flower, which is beautiful and remains *unaffected* despite the ugly marshes it lives in. Likewise, our meditative practice inculcates in us a sense of dispassion and detachment for the superficial, material world we live in. As the lotus does, we rise above the mundane into higher *awareness*, and thus bloom to our fullest potential.

Chapter Thirteen

Essence of Life

for the breath is well tamed if
it is held at the tip of the nose;
if you hold it in your navel,
sickness will have no hold on you;
and if it is kept in the toes,
your body will become shining bright!
—Yoga Darshana Upanishad

According to an ancient parable, there was once a great convention of all the senses of man...to decide who would be the King. To gain power and importance, the senses came dressed in their finest apparel, as each of them competed with the other. The sense of *sight* was beautifully adorned in brilliant colors; the sense of *sound* wore jewelry that chimed like clear silver bells. *Sight, sound* and all the others argued for leadership, and each sense attempted to out-shine the other.

Only the *breath* remained unseen in his common and ordinary attire. He soon grew tired of the senseless arguments and quietly slipped out unnoticed. Suddenly, the beauty and brilliance of all the other senses began to fade. Recognizing the ultimate power that *breath* had, the other senses begged him to stay. They crowned him the King, and paid their full respect to his sovereignty. Such is the power of breath *awareness*!

This thousand year old parable is as relevant today as it was then, perhaps even more so. We have become increasingly sensory-dependent on our fast-paced modern culture and high-tech society. Even for relaxation, we look to external means, like the use of sophisticated biofeedback methods and computerized virtual reality. In this way, we become a slave to our senses and lose touch with our own resources. Because we are externally influenced, we remain unaware of our inner strength.

I comment on how refreshed Nicole and Bryan look after their two-week honeymoon in Cayman, an island I remember as one of great beauty: lagoons of still and clear blue water, crystal sand, exotic underwater life—an ideal place to absolve ourselves in nature, and dive within. Nicole relates that all her worries seemed to dissolve when they went scuba diving.

Like "walking by the still waters," as said in Psalms 23:2, meditation is an immersion within our inner selves. The deeper we submerge ourselves, the more silence and stillness we experience.

When Nicole and Bryan tried to recreate this peaceful sensation above land, they discovered that focusing was harder than they thought.

"My breathing was uncoordinated, and I couldn't still my train of thoughts," Nicole admits.

Breath, I explain, is the *physical* counterpart of the mind. As it conjures up images in the mind, it is essentially the mind in action. The sight of an accident, the sound of thunder, the scent of a lover's perfume...all of these things create internal dialogues in our mind and *direct* the way we breathe. In each of the above situations, our breathing becomes rapid and irregular.

Similarly, it becomes fast and erratic when we are angry, and when we hyperventilate, anxiety settles in. It becomes shallow with frequent sighs when we experience depression or withdrawal. However, our inner turmoil is quietened when we stop to take a deep breath, and is slow and regular when we are calm. This clearly illustrates the *two-way* mind-breath connection.

For most of us, breath is spontaneous and is taken for granted. Like our heart beat, our breathing is involuntary. So even if we "forget" to breathe, our body switches on "auto-pilot" and continues to breathe for us. We usually do not become aware of the breath unless we develop conditions, like asthma or emphysema. But this powerful tool—however neglected it is—amazingly allows us to achieve self-control.

"Then how does the breath connect our mind and body?" Bryan questions.

Just like the AM or FM radio waves that transmit the music, the breath is the principal carrier of *prana*. By changing the *Amplitude* or *Frequency* of breath, we can *modulate* the flow of this subtle life force.

Breath distributes the *prana*, or *aliveness*, therefore providing the vital link between the mind and body. The breath affects the flow of *prana*—fluid-like energies—in the extensive network of *nadis*. Delivering *pranic* force, it provides access to the internal organs.

Prana is perceived as an air element and creates movement, pulsation, vibration and *aliveness*. As we have learned in earlier sessions, *prana* is the interface between the *subtle* and *gross bodies*. Located in the *subtle body*—at the confluence of *nadis*—are those seven *chakras*, or centers of *awareness*. The *chakras* act as transformers, directing the energy flow from the *nadis* to the major organ systems. By controlling the flow of *prana*—and *prana's* relationship to the *chakras*—the breath influences our *awareness*. *Prana* is *not* the breath itself however, for it is the vital energy that sustains *all* living things by water, food, air and sunlight.

Yoga science recognizes the relationship that exists between *prana* and the mind; there is an inherent link between *chit*, or *awareness*, and *prana*, or *aliveness*. By controlling the breathing process through the technique of *pranayama*, those who meditate become masters of the mind. As said in the *Yoga Sutra*, "suspend the *prana*, and the modifications of *chit*, or consciousness will cease." Let us now explore this relationship between breathing and our "inner world."

Western scientists have known for years that our breath influences the fluctuations in our pulse through the *autonomic nervous system*. Inhalation stimulates the *sympathetic limb*, speeding up the pulse. Exhalation slows the heartbeat by increasing activity in the *parasympathetic limb*. This influence is so strong that by controlling our breath, we can manipulate our "inner world." By uncovering the secrets of breathing, we are able to overcome emotional overload and "tame" our primitive urges.

The breath guides our neuromotor activities—the sensory and motor functions of the body. Unlike any other process in the body, the breath has a dual function; its uniqueness lies in the fact that it has a relationship to *both* voluntary or *sensory-motor*, and involuntary or *autonomic nervous system*. This dual connection gives us *conscious* control of *involuntary* autonomic processes, and thus is the secret to our internal well being.

Like the yogis who could selectively regulate their heartbeat and lower their blood pressure, we also can learn to achieve these powers through breath control or *pranayama*.

The right and left sub-divisions of the *vagus nerve*—the tenth cranial nerve—coursing through the chest cavity sense the exact movement of the lungs through a reflex mechanism. The nerve receptors in the lungs convey the extent of breath expansion to our "inner world" via the *vagus nerve*.

The signals are predominantly *sympathetic* when we breathe from the chest, which often convey to us a sense of danger. Our body's emergency breathing system then activates the "flight or fight response" regardless of whether or not there is actual threat. Subconsciously, we set off a perpetual alarm reaction when we habitually breathe from the chest. On the surface, we may appear to be relaxed and calm, but underneath we are exhibiting a *chronic stress* response.

The majority of our breathing patterns are characteristic of our emotional states. For instance, "coronary-prone" behavior characterized by *time urgency* and *hostility* has a distinctive *mid-cycle pause* in breath that occurs after the inhalation and right before the exhalation. Uneven and irregular breathing leads to autonomic imbalance, stress or chaos in the "inner world," and over a period of time, becomes significantly detrimental.

Like hypertension and heart disease, this latency eventually becomes overt. If modern medicine can spend billions of dollars treating breath-related illnesses of all kinds, why does it not pay attention to the breath *itself*? We cannot live without the power of breath, yet this remarkable essence of life remains unnoticed.

Smooth diaphragmatic breathing, by *parasympathetic* stimulation, has a calming effect and induces relaxation deep within. This is the access to the *autonomic nervous system*, the key to eliminating stress, creating harmony in the "inner world" and taking control of our health.

"I know that when I'm stressed out, I actually forget to breathe," Nicole says. "How do we develop such bad habits in the first place?"

Like other negative habits in life, chest breathing is something we eventually acquire. We are born with the inherent "know-how" of diaphragmatic breathing, yet we "forget." In the womb, the nostrils are not yet operative, and the lungs are dormant. The *prana* flows from the mother to the fetus through the umbilical cord. After birth, the breath is the first thing that regulates all the bodily activity as the lungs begin to operate. With the first cry of the newborn, *prana* delivery switches from a fluid to an air medium.

Watch a newborn baby asleep in its crib. There is little or no movement of the chest; only the abdomen moves rhythmically up and down. Even when infants show other signs of distress, they still maintain diaphragmatic breathing.

As we grow, we develop unhealthy habits that interfere with our innate breathing patterns. Society plays a significant role in this shift from breathing with the belly, to the chest. In most of Western civilization, a flat abdomen is considered an attractive attribute for both males and females. Pulling in our stomachs, or wearing tight clothing creates tension in the abdominal muscles. The diaphragm loses its freedom of movement, and we rely on chest breathing.

Bodybuilders and soldiers exaggerate chest expansion by chest breathing, which inhibits diaphragmatic excursion and puts extra pressure on the heart. This encourages a constant "fight or flight" response.

In the average chest-breather, a state of *chronic arousal* causes constriction in the peripheral blood vessels, leading to hypertension. A decrease of the heart function follows as more blood is translocated centrally. Breathing diaphragmatically by allowing more room, releases this "load" or chronic strain from the heart muscle and lowers the blood pressure.

Psychological trauma during our childhood may be another reason we unknowingly develop the habit of chest breathing. For instance, when a child is scolded, the physiological response is a tightening of the abdominal muscles, preventing breath in the diaphragm. Like most of life's lessons, what we learn in childhood continues to have an extremely powerful effect on us as adults. Our breathing habits are no exception.

Improper posture also restricts the natural diaphragmatic rhythm, forcing us to rely on the chest. All traditions of self-mastery that have evolved from yoga—martial arts, ballet and other forms of dance—use correct posture and a variety of breathing techniques to develop inner balance, strength, coordination and self-control.

"Movement never lies. It is a barometer telling the state of the soul's weather to all who can read it." Those are the words of dance legend Martha Graham, who understood physical dance as the body's expression of emotional energy. The *aliveness* of a body, like that of a dancer, is conveyed through a variety of movement and sequence. The *prana* is the principal performer who guides the *corps de ballet* of body-mind-soul with its ethereal essence.

Ballet is a world of precise choreography, the smooth, unbroken sequence of steps and placement. We are enchanted by the magical flow of movement on the stage, which is far removed from disruptive, everyday life. Now imagine that the ballet has gone unrehearsed, and the choreography is haphazard so the whole effect is unsettling.

The same is true with our breath. Like dancing, the ideal breathing motion is like a smooth and unbroken wave, when the breath is even and uninterrupted; it is recorded as a perfect *sine wave*. Research indicates that, given the bad breathing habits we acquire, very few people register this type of breath flow pattern without the proper training. And how can we reap the benefits of meditation when our breath control is at fault?

Irregular, uneven breath creates turbulent thought waves on the surface of the mind, and makes it hard to sail through meditation.

Smooth Sailing

When we practice breathing, our body should remain as calm and silent as the deep ocean. Like the throb and movement of life beneath an ocean, the soft thump of the heart vibrates with each breath we take.

Lying down in a relaxed posture, we close our eyes and breathe in and out through our nose. As we concentrate on our breathing, our abdomen should expand and contract with each breath, as if there was a balloon under the diaphragm. Placing our hands on the abdomen to chart our rhythm, we fill and deflate the balloon, our hands *rising* with the *inhalation* and *falling* to the *exhalation*, like waves in the sea. (Fig.12)

The breath cycle has to be very smooth, without any pause or tur-bulence. Both inhalation and exhalation should be about the same length and have the same "pressure." Breathing should always be gentle, seemingly without effort. For simply relearning the natural

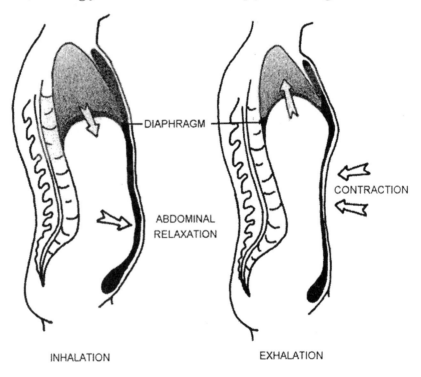

FIGURE 12. DIAPHRAGMATIC BREATHING

rhythm, it is only necessary to fill or empty the lungs at comfort level.

The in and out-going breaths represent two guards who watch over the fortress of life. When they are well coordinated, our defenses are strong. But when the guards are disorganized, we are vulnerable to the enemy. Most of us take it for granted that they are doing their jobs, and seldom inspect them. It does not occur to us that they are often poorly trained and inefficient, and many a time polluted with tobacco smoke!

Our breathing habits not only reflect our state of being, but also have a profound effect on all the functions of the body and mind. An even, quiet diaphragmatic breath passing through the nose is the *ideal*, but most of us unknowingly deviate from this breathing pattern.

If the diaphragm is "frozen," the breath is shallow and limited to the chest; we feel fatigued, anxious and easily stressed. Mouth breathing, as a result of nasal obstruction—like during a cold or sinus infection—makes us breathe in jerks or with gaps. Pausing between inhalation and exhalation disrupts the flow of vital energy. Most of us never realize what a drain this "unnatural breathing" is on the life force!

How can we fortify the defenses in the citadel of life? The secret lies in the changing of the guards—at the end of inhalation and exhalation. The process should be a smooth transition of in and out, a subtle merging of both. By maintaining a gentle tension in the abdominal muscles throughout the exhalation, and phasing out this tension into the beginning of inhalation, helps narrow the unwanted *gap*.

Once an even and equal breathing pattern is established, we can gradually lengthen the exhalation period to be twice as long as the inhalation. A good start is to count to four on the inhalation, and eight on the exhalation to achieve a 1:2 ratio of the breath cycle, but any comfortable count, such as three to six, is acceptable as long as the ratio is maintained.

By adjusting the ratio, we influence the *autonomic nervous system* to our advantage. The *extended* exhalation not only induces relaxation by stimulating the *parasympathetic*, but also helps tone down the *sympathetic* arousal emphasized during inhalation.

The art of diaphragmatic breathing is easy to learn and should be practiced for at least ten minutes twice a day. By cultivating breath *awareness*, we gradually replace the unnatural chest breathing habit with diaphragmatic breathing.

I tell Nicole and Bryan to take a few moments and imagine their breath as a wave, which is slowly and steadily undulating from the diaphragm to the lungs and back again.

"I feel invigorated, like I was granted a new supply of energy," Nicole says. "No dose of Valium will ever equal that feeling."

And that is only after a few minutes of deep breathing! Just imagine a whole day's worth of proper technique that provides us with energy we so often lack when faced with stress or anxiety. If we know how to breathe, we do not become so tired by the end of the day.

Like the tortoise—who, by slow and steady conservation of energy won the race over the quicker, but easily—exhausted hare—the breath becomes the most magnificent source of empowerment in our fast paced society.

Walking to Exhale

Walking outdoors, on an inside track or even on a treadmill is the most convenient and practical type of physical fitness I can think of. It not only conditions the heart and lungs, but also alleviates muscle tension, stimulates digestion and aids in elimination. At a brisk pace, it burns as many calories as jogging and does not put extra stress on the joints.

When we incorporate diaphragmatic breathing with walking, it leaves us ever more refreshed and energized. Observing the breath as we walk is *meditation in action*—it clears our mind of mental chatter, and activates our abdominal muscles while emphasizing the heat and vitality of breath in the navel center. Visualize the navel center leading us forward instead of the chest or head, and monitor the length of inhalation and exhalation. Using our steps to count the duration of breaths, we will gradually be able to adjust the ratio so that both phases become equal in length.

Once we have cultivated basic abdominal technique, we can now try to lengthen the exhalation so that it is twice as long as the inhalation. It takes time to build such a capacity, however, and if we feel strained or overly exerted, it is wise to return to a more comfortable level of breathing.

The breath, in fact, is one of the most important components of yoga, martial arts, ballet and other forms of dance. Breath carries us through the convolutions of *asanas* or postures and a dancer through the routine, as it can do the same for the average person who applies breathing technique during exercise.

Life Insurance

Yoga wisdom does not measure a human life in years, but by the number of breaths. Yogis believe that a person who breathes shallowly—in short, sharp gasps—is also apt to live a short life, and that each individual has a fixed amount of breaths in one lifetime. To breathe deeply and slowly is to optimize the length and vitality of life. In fact, the *ideal* human life is comprised of a total of 946,080,000 breaths—a full 120-year life span!

Through their keen observation, the yogis observed the lifespan of different animals, and concluded that the slower the frequency of breath, the longer the lifespan. For instance, a monkey breathes thirty-two times a minute and lives about sixteen years. A turtle breathes five times a minute, and lives 500 years. In between is the average human being, who breathes sixteen times a minute and has a life expectancy of about 75 years.

If we breathe from the chest, we breathe approximately 24,000 times per day, at a rate of 16 to 20 breaths per minute. Breathing efficiency significantly improves by 50% when we start breathing from the diaphragm, 12,000 times a day, at the rate of 8 to 10 breaths!

With an increase of breathing frequency, we deplete vital energy reserves, contributing to our wear and tear. Increased stress or strain on our system over time reduces our longevity. However, we can reverse the aging process by slowing down the rate and the length of the breath through diligent practice of *pranayama.*

If we grasp the basic idea of expansion and contraction—the "Cosmic Breath"—then we can see harmony in *all* the levels of existence. At the microcosmic level, an instinctive pulsation is present in the sperm and ovum, which sustains the organism before it even breathes for the first time.

The evolution or expansion of *awareness*—or the devolution or contraction—is the same phenomenon. The entire universe itself is swelling, so to speak, and after a certain point, it will coalesce again—all the planets, solar systems and galaxies will converge—only to explode all over again! This cycle of creation and dissolution in yoga philosophy, is described as the "Big Bang"—the inhalation—and the "Big Crunch"—the exhalation—of the cosmos, as viewed by astronomers. Hence, one can spend virtual lifetimes exploring and understanding the subtleties and implications of the breathing process.

How we proceed from taming our breath to controlling the cosmic energy of *prana*, and thus the lifespan, is illustrated by the following story:

There was once a king's minister who was imprisoned at the top of a tall tower after he fell into his majesty's disgrace. One night, the minister's faithful wife brought her husband a long rope, some strong twine, string, a silken thread, a beetle and some honey. Bewildered by his strange requests, she nevertheless did as she was told. The minister then asked her to tie the silken thread to the beetle; to smear honey on its tentacles and to then set the insect on the wall with its head pointed toward the tower. Enticed by the sweet smell of honey, the beetle slowly made its way to the top of the tower, pulling the silken thread along with it. The minister took hold of the thread, and asked his wife to tie the string to the other end of the thread. From the thread, he then drew up the string, using it to retrieve the strong twine. Then with the twine, he drew up the rope, and descended to freedom.

Within our own bodies, the *breath* is like the silken thread. By breath control, we learn to skillfully grasp the string of the *nerve impulses*. From these, we capture the strong twine of our *thoughts*, and finally retrieve the rope of *prana*. And through our connection to this cosmic energy—the very essence of life—we are able to insure our ultimate freedom.

Chapter Fourteen

Celestial Connection

The moon and the sun unite
within your body when the breath
resides in the meeting place
of the two nadis.
—Yoga Darshana Upanishad

A s I wait in my office for Nicole, Bryan and my four patients to arrive for our session, I take a minute to contemplate the changing season outside my window. It is one of those early evenings in March, when the snow has mostly melted from the gathering strength of the day's sun and tiny buds are already beginning to show on the trees. Spring flirts with the air, coaxing it with warm breezes and the first hint of fragrance.

As the sun's rays are just beginning to fade away, a soft, white sliver appears, marking the last quarter moon of winter. By the time my meditators join me, there is still a crimson hint of sun left in the sky. On the other side the moon rises, glowing brighter as dusk descends.

When the group arrives, we gather to look out the window at the very same sky the ancient yoga masters must have seen when they explained the bond between the sun, the moon and the breath to their disciples.

"It's so enchanting, the way the sun and moon are together like that," Erin exclaims. "I should know, I've spent many sleepless nights just watching the sky."

"While on a silent retreat in Hilton Head, one of the things Debra and I did was meditate," Mike says. "The experience was so memorable because of the light changing in the sky."

"You know, I could never separate day and night because of all the long hours I worked," Joe adds. "Meditating has made me appreciate nature."

Unknowingly, they have just echoed what yogis for thousands of years have believed about the inherent connection between nature and physiology: the phases of the sun and moon are like the cycles of "celestial breath" occurring in the universe, or macrocosm.

These phases epitomize how the world is constantly breathing. With each interlude of darkness into light, and each journey from new moon to full, there is a breath. Life on earth is regulated by these processes, as is the entire cosmos.

As the sun sets and the moon rises, and when the moonlight again gives way to the sunshine, a similar, natural transition is reflected in the nostrils. Ideally, one nostril is flowing more freely than the other is, but both take turns being dominant and open. The alternating nasal cycle of right and left nostrils is the microcosmic counterpart.

Yoga science maintains that there is a natural cycle of alternating nasal dominance in each one of us. Validated by Western scientists, nostril predominance—one over the other—occurs every ninety minutes or so. But because we no longer live in a natural environment, a perfect cycle is exceedingly rare. Our modern, fast-paced lifestyle and deadlines deviate the pattern, however. If we utilize the knowledge of the nasal cycle—like the yogis—we are able to live in a state of external and internal harmony, as well.

Animals do not have a nose in the sense that we do. Not usually perceived as a neurological organ, our nose, in fact, originates in the brain and has a more sophisticated function. Yet most of us think the nose is merely a set of passages for the lungs. Man is actually unique in that he is equipped with such an intricate feature.

Given its strategic location near the "inner world," the nose is actually the "switchboard" for the entire nervous system. The most vital link between our own body and the universal energy is the breath, and the nose provides this access.

The nerve endings in the nose provide our sense of smell, but the organ is also the only part of the *limbic system* with direct contact to the outside world. Our own nasal cycle—the alternation of the right and left nostrils—is able to synchronize all human functions by its link to breath outside the body. While we may worry about the size and shape of our nose, we seldom consider what goes on inside it until we develop a cold or a sinus infection and are forced to breathe with the mouth.

The roof of the mouth forms the floor of the nasal cavity, while the roof of the nasal cavity forms the floor of the brain. By its link to the *olfactory lobe*, the nose is in direct contact with the "microchip" of the brain, or *hypothalamus*, a part of the *limbic system*, and is placed strategically near the *autonomic nervous system* and the *pituitary gland*.

The *sympathetic* and *parasympathetic* commands influence nasal dominance of one over the other. When the right nostril or *pingala nadi* is active, there is *sympathetic* arousal. In contrast, when the left nostril or *ida nadi* flow predominates, there is *parasympathetic* inhibition.

Activating the master *pituitary gland,* or "orchestra conductor" of the metabolism by directing hormonal flow is the *ida nadi.* The *pingala* interacts with the *hypothalamus,* affecting blood pressure, body temperature, biorhythms and our emotions. The *sushumna* connects to the *corpus callosm*—the bridge between the left and right *cerebral hemispheres*—and enables a balance of the two halves of the brain. It also pierces every *chakra* in the *subtle body,* and finally terminates in the *crown chakra,* or *sahasara.*

Within our subtle body, *prana* moves along these invisible pathways. Each nostril imparts a particular quality to the *prana* that passes through the *nadis,* or energy networks. Two primary *nadis* originating from the base of the spine correspond to the right and left nostrils: the *pingala nadi,* or "solar nadi" which terminates in the right nostril, and the *ida nadi,* or "lunar nadi" which ends in the left.

The *sushumna nadi,* or central channel, is only activated when both nostrils are flowing equally. Normally, this occurs at dawn and dusk. At these defining moments, the *prana* moves uninhibited through this central channel. From its abode at the base of the spine, *kundalini* energy can only then ascend to meet *sahasara* when this central channel is open.

Because the mind naturally converges, these are times most conducive for inner pursuits. Living in harmony with nature, we can engage in meditation at sunrise and sunset. Thus, a blissful state is within reach.

Despite the fact that they lead to the brain, the openings in the nose are more circuitous than entirely straight. These winding passageways are called *turbinates*, and are responsible for the circulation and compression of air in the nose. The wind speed within the nostrils can reach 20 miles an hour when we are breathing quietly, and during vigorous exercise, the velocity can increase substantially. Outside, a 200 mile an hour wind can destroy a community, but the same amount of inner turbulence is simply the equivalent of good aerobic exercise!

The air flowing through the nose stimulates the various nerve endings. As blood flow shifts through the nose, the nasal passages—lined with erectile tissue—alternately swell and shrink. The continuous engorgement and shrinking of the nostrils establishes an infinite variety of flow patterns, creating a "switchboard" effect for the entire nervous system. If we alter this neuro-stimulation, we are able to influence—for better or for worse—all other bodily mechanisms.

The only other erectile tissues in the body are the sexual organs, and the nipples. Being newlyweds, Nicole and Bryan are probably struck not only by Cupid's arrow, but also by a condition known as "honeymoon nose." The sexual urge is strongest at the beginning of a relationship, so our nose is ultra-sensitive.

Such stimulation in the *limbic system* increases the production of *pheromones*, individual secretions that are perceived by others, and serve as individual "scents." Evidence suggests that we are attracted to certain people, and are repelled by others because of the *pheromones* they release. Several experiments conducted on groups of men of all ages show that the majority of them prefer distinct scents to others. The smell of doughnuts, bread baking and lavender seem to entice them the most! Taking this into account, the cosmetic industry has capitalized on our tendencies toward particular scents, and advertises their perfumes and colognes with sex-oriented labels.

An active right nostril is characteristic of the male archetype: aggressive, assertive and dominant. Such a male behavior pattern is more natural when the right nostril takes precedence. In yoga, the masculine right nostril is associated with the Sun, the solar planets Mars and Saturn, and the corresponding days—Sunday, Tuesday and Saturday, respectively. It is referred to as the "solar principle" in all its active and fiery glory. The inhaled air through the right side creates *tapas*, or heat in the center of the body, providing energy and functioning power to the muscles and organs.

The feminine counterpart is found in the left nostril, or "lunar principle." It is associated with the Moon and the lunar planets, Mercury, Jupiter and Venus, and the days of Monday, Wednesday, Thursday and Friday. Like cool water, the air exhaled from the left has a calming effect on us; there is a decrease in metabolism as our body relaxes. When the left nostril is open, we are naturally more receptive, and less likely to engage in activity.

Learning about nostril dominance and its significance is like trying to relate to someone who only speaks sign language. At first, each action and gesture the person makes is a mystery, but through careful observation, his or her actions become familiar, even meaningful. Through their personal experimentation, the yogis have discovered the cross-linkage between the right nostril and left brain activity, and the left nostril with the right hemisphere.

Contemporary neurobiologists also discovered that both cerebral and nostril dominance can occur at the same time. Just as we are not entirely right or left-brained, the airflow in the nostrils of a healthy person shifts from one nostril to the other over a period of time.

The hemispheres of the brain are the tools of the mind, and the nostrils indicate which part of the brain is predominant at a given time. Right nostril/left hemisphere dominance indicates that we are taking action, working, exercising, problem solving, while left nostril/right hemisphere dominance represents the rest phase. Research has been conducted as to how some forms of depression might relate to overactivity of the left nostril, and excessive airflow in the right may be associated with hyperactivity. They have not fully grasped the implications, however. When we become more *aware* of the connection between our brain and nose, we can then start applying what we know—gradually and consistently—to our daily activities.

Yoga science has always maintained that the airflow through the two nostrils is quite distinct. What serves as the "barometer"of this cerebral dominance are the nostrils; they may help us anticipate our response to a given circumstance. Under the influence of different hemispheres, we handle the same situations differently. Once we understand this, we can make optimum use of energy by performing actions best suited for the dominant hemisphere.

Incoming breath through the *right* nostril cools the *right* hemisphere, so the *left* side of the brain is activated. The *opposite* effect is achieved with the intake of breath through the *left* nostril. The calm, collected demeanor and internal harmony of a meditator is representative of such skillfulness. By becoming "breath friendly," we can also overcome the burdens of our emotional overload. This skill becomes our "power within," so we are not as often the helpless victims of emotional states.

It is potentially valuable to know that when our right nostril is open, we are more disposed to be eating and digesting food, writing, teaching, playing sports or engaging in other outward activities. In each of these pursuits, we are externalizing our *awareness*, or moving out into the world. In contrast, when the left nostril is dominant, we internalize as we listen to music or lectures, or read. These qualities ascribed to the nostrils are not absolute, but relative broad concepts. Though they are not set "traits," they help us to consult our own breathing patterns.

There are several good reasons for becoming more *aware* of nostril dominance. Breathing predominantly through one nostril influences both body and mind, and our daily situations. We all have bad days, and when things do not work out, we wonder what we could have done differently. Do we even know how often we work against ourselves because we are not *aware* of our internal rhythms? Realizing which nostril is dominant, we can make necessary adjust-ments.

For example, right nostril dominance is preferable when digesting a meal since it requires abundant energy. Eating with our left nos-tril open is likely to be a less satisfying experience; this impercep-tible difference is actually telling the body that it is not ready to metabolize and assimilate food.

The body needs nourishment and our mind is pre-disposed ac-cordingly. If our right nostril happens to be open and dominant, we will get to replenish our energy stores, and enjoy ourselves as well. We look forward to eating lunch if we have not eaten since breakfast. On the other hand, if we had a mid-morning snack, and our left nostril is open, we do not anticipate the lunch hour as much. If we eat just because it is "time" to eat, the meal is not as nourishing. Our digestion will be sluggish, and energy levels will plummet earlier, even if what we ate was wholesome.

In this way, the *body*, *breath* and *mind* are like three sails. When all are unfurled properly, the ship sails smoothly. But if even one is improperly rigged, the ship is unable to breeze through, and sails off-course. By skillful coordination, we are able to navigate with ease.

"Since we live in such a fast-paced world, such coordination is sometimes difficult," Mike says.

True as that may be, we can consciously *choose* not to eat when the right nostril is closed, although other activities can not easily be postponed. For instance, we may be scheduled to make a busi-ness presentation in an adversarial situation, and find that the left nostril is dominant.

The answer is *shifting* to the preferred nostril. A practical way to achieve right nostril dominance in that kind of situation is taking a brisk walk, even up and down a flight of stairs. Another simple method of altering dominance is applying pressure underneath the opposite arm with the use of a small pillow or a towel. The nostril will usually shift in about 3 to 5 minutes, but may take as long as 15 minutes. After an evening meal, it is also helpful to lie down on the left side to open the right nostril, and enhance digestion.

Erin inquires how we can tell which nostril is dominant, or open. I demonstrate that if we carefully watch our breath, we notice that one nostril seems to be flowing more freely than the other is: this is the active or dominant nostril. This is true at almost any time of day or night. The opposite nostril, which may seem stuffy or ob-structed, is passive. We are able to observe this phenomenon in several ways. By inhaling and exhaling deeply two or three times, focusing all of our attention on the nostrils, we can decipher which one feels more open.

We can visualize this same process by exhaling over a small mirror held directly under the nostrils, as the active nostril will leave a larger spot of moisture.

Nicole is curious about how to figure this out when we have a chronic sinus condition or cold. I am glad she asked, since millions suffer from sinus afflictions. Interestingly, yoga provides a simple and inexpensive solution to keep them at bay.

Passage to Inner World

Administering a nasal wash cleanses and rejuvenates the lining in the nose, alleviating nasal congestion, preventing infection and eventually eliminating sinus headaches. It clears nasal passages, allowing us to breathe more easily through the nose, and not the mouth. Open mouth breathing, as in allergies or sleep apnea, oc-curs because of partial blocks in the nasal passages.

And though most of us find the thought of water in the nostrils unpleasant—like getting water in our nose while swimming or bathing—a daily nasal wash with saline solution is extremely healthful. The only difficult part of the technique is our attitude; you can tell by the look on people's faces that most of us consider water inside the nose disgusting. What is disgusting is that we walk around with excess mucous inside the nasal passages, carrying it around like a personal treasure!

Using lukewarm saline water to clean the nose is an ancient yoga practice called *jala neti*, or "water cleansing." Though once popular, this age-old technique has fallen out of favor among the modern medical circles with the advent of over-the-counter decongestants.

To begin, we fill an eight-ounce *neti-pot* (a pot with a spout) or a similar kind of dispenser (complete with nozzle or spout) with lukewarm water, and add approximately one-eighth teaspoon of iodine-free, kosher or sea salt. The water should be as salty as tears, since the salt draws out the impurities built up in the nasal cavity.

Tilting the head back slightly, we bring the spout to the nostrils. Keeping our throat, mouth and jaw relaxed, we tilt the glass and inhale just enough to pour water into our nasal passages. Then dropping our head, we exhale with a gentle force through both nostrils, letting the water drain back out. After a little practice, we will be able to tilt our head back and to one side, bringing the water in through the upper nostril and letting it drain out through the other.

The sensitive erectile tissue and the abundantly exposed nerve endings of the nasal passages make a very unique interface between the *physical* and *subtle body*. Maintenance of this intricate "gateway to the mind" not only alleviates nasal problems, but also insures optimum health in the long run.

Bryan is skeptical about how we can actually manipulate the nostrils, and gain control over our entire system.

In our own bio-computer, the brain is the *hardware* and the mind is the *software*. The *mouse* that manipulates this mind-brain interface is the nose itself!

Ebb and Flow

To determine which nostril is active, we close our eyes and sit comfortably with our head, neck and torso in alignment. If the right nostril is active, we press our ring finger against the left nostril, exhaling to a mental count of six. We then inhale immediately through the same nostril for a count of six. (Fig. 13)

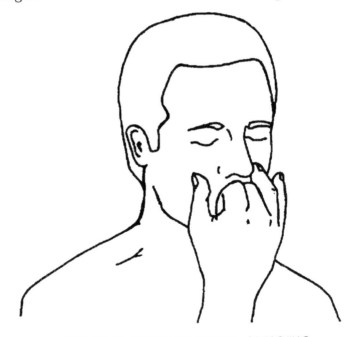

FIGURE 13. ALTERNATE NOSTRIL BREATHING.

Next, we gently press the thumb against the right nostril, closing it off, and at the same time, relieving the pressure on the left nostril. We can exhale for a count of six, and then inhale again for another count of six through the left nostril. Now we press the ring finger against the left nostril, closing off the flow of breath again, while simultaneously releasing the pressure from the thumb on the right nostril. Exhale and inhale for a count of six through the right nostril. This completes one round, and usually we need about sixteen rounds to complete the entire exercise.

The counting demands that we focus our attention on regulating our breath, so this exercise is especially profitable for someone who is stressed or agitated. After we practice for a few weeks or months, complete concentration on the breath is a lot easier without the distraction of counting. There is then a subtle, inward flow of the mind.

As long as diligence, patience and moderation accompany practice, even practicing for five to ten minutes at a time is beneficial. Over a period of weeks or months, we will notice that much of our stress is slowly shifting in the direction of balance, stability and integration. More advanced exercise, however, requires constant, competent guidance.

One of the most beautiful aspects of yoga is that we learn by practicing and experiencing techniques, not just simply reading about, or studying them.

Improper breathing creates dysfunction and turbulence in both the body and mind. We lose approximately 15% of our physical strength when we breathe through the mouth.

Research conducted by Dr. Alan Hymes reports that over 75% of heart attack victims seldom breathe correctly through their noses. Nearly all of those mouth-breathers snore while sleeping, while 84% of them develop sleep apnea, a major contributor of heart disease, and a potentially life-threatening condition that strikes the central nervous system.

Dr. Maurice Cottle, an ENT specialist in Chicago, associated a mid-cycle pause in the breathing pattern (after the exhalation and before the inhalation) with heart attacks. When this pause occurs in sleep—usually lasting for 30 seconds or longer—it is characterized by loud, open-mouthed snoring, with periodic silences between each snore. The sound is created by the obstruction of air at the larynx: the passages in the nose remain closed, so the breath is forced out of the mouth. The oxygen imbalance puts a strain on the heart and prevents the excretion of carbon dioxide through the lungs.

A chronic accumulation of what should be exhaled out of our system, but is not, hardens the arteries and increases the constriction of blood vessels surrounding the heart, increasing the risk of hypertension.

Sleep apnea is corrected by diaphragmatic breathing. Closing the mouth stops the snoring, and the nasal passages are reactivated. Respiratory efficiency improves as soon as the breath becomes even. This literally "takes a load off the chest," as balance is restored. Deep, diaphragmatic breathing, as in *pranayama*, utilizes both openings of the nose, so that the flow of breath is balanced and even. As a result, we can learn to regulate our body chemistry so that each and every process—physical and mental—is working the way it should.

Pranayama is a single Sanksrit word defined by two: *Prana* means a subtle life force which gives energy to the mind and body, and *yama* signifies the voluntary effort to control and direct this *prana*. "Exhale and retain the breath" defines the process of *pranayama*. If we breathe out and then refuse to inhale again, we will soon experience what *prana* really is. Very quickly, we are forced to take another breath, and what makes us take the next breath after holding it for so long is *prana*.

Yoga is *experiential* by nature, so no definition can ever truly contain the essence of *prana*. If we want to know what total absorption of the mind feels like, we can simply exhale and suspend the breathing. During this time, we can think of nothing but the breath, and even a few seconds without it can feel like hours. Our mind becomes quiet when we hold our breath, however, since it is the movement of *prana* that enables our mind to think in the first place.

In deep meditation, the breath naturally becomes suspended for a short period of time, and in this brief instance, *pranayama* is revealed to us. It effectively and efficiently removes the dark veil of ignorance that so often covers our inner light. The *prana* is so intimately related to the mind that the breath will undoubtedly become restless when we are angry or emotionally upset. That is one reason we should cultivate a positive attitude in life, and overcome negative and destructive tendencies or behaviors. *Pranayama* is aimed primarily at the suspension of mental activity in order to bring about a tranquil state of mind.

Like the silent union of sunset and moonrise on the horizon, the control of breath within creates the connection between the solar and lunar principles...and the "dawning" of meditation ensues.

Chapter Fifteen

Cosmic Rhythms

And God said, "Let there be light." And there was light.
And God saw the light, it was good: And God divided
the Light from the darkness. And God called the light
day and darkness, he called night.
And there was evening and there was morning, one day.
—Genesis 1

Outside my window, the image of a vanishing sun and encroaching moon epitomize for me the interconnectedness of everything in nature. Neither fights each other for space in the sky, nor does one try to reign over the other. Instead, the two forces of nature blend like the sequence of decrescending and crescending notes in a *raga*, or melodic composition. There is a rhythm to the movement, like the fading of day into night, and the lifting of light out of darkness, that is enchanting.

We mark the annual progress of the seasons by the springtime buds on the trees, summertime's green foliage, the rusting of autumn leaves and the winter frost. We observe the changes in temperature, and the length of days, turning our clocks ahead when the weather gets warmer and turning back time at the first sign of chill. We watch the sky in wonder, tracking the path of migrating birds who instinctively know what time to fly away, and when to return.

What then accounts for the perpetual seasonal cycles? Our planet revolves around the sun once every year, and the *tilt* of its axis is responsible for seasonal changes. Since it is not vertically straight, but tilted sideways instead, the earth's two hemispheres alternate between receiving direct sun rays in summer, and obliquely in winter. So when it is hot and summery here in the United States, it is cold and wintry in farther regions of Australia and New Zealand.

In addition to annual events like the seasons, there are daily fluctuations. The distinction between night and day is the most pervasive—we experience light and then darkness as the earth *spins* on its axis, exposing us to, and hiding us from, the sun. The time it takes to complete a revolution—give or take the odd second—is twenty-four hours, or what is known as the *solar day.* As a result, many aspects of our environment demonstrate a similar twenty-four hour rhythm.

The earth orbits the sun and the moon orbits the earth. Because of the moon's gravitational pull, two large bulges of water appear in the ocean and cause high tides—one facing the moon and the other turned away from the source. The time it takes for the moon to appear at equal heights above the horizon is twenty-four hours and fifty minutes—what is known as the *lunar day.* So with respect to the *solar* time, the tides wash upon the shore later each day.

Life above sea level senses day and night by the movement of the sun and moon. In contrast, the creatures just below the water can not measure day and night by sunshine or moonlight. They sense these cosmic rhythms by the ebb and flow of the tide. The deep underwater occupants of the dark recesses, however, escape these rhythmic infuences and are effected only by debris, which falls from above to the ocean floor.

Our bodies are seventy percent water, directly correlating with the water content of the earth. Just as the moon influences the tidal waves in the ocean, it affects the fluids in our system as well. The moon changes bi-monthly, or twice a month, affecting our mood cycles and body chemistry, which is a common observation. Evidence also cites that those who suffer from manic-depression show more volatile behavior around the ascending lunar cycle, or full moon. Yet when the moon is waning, and becoming new again, withdrawal predominates in such individuals. The correlation is powerful, so much so that the term *lunacy* is derived from *luna*, or moon.

Though the yogis acquired their great knowledge through nature, science has only recently begun to recognize the full impact of cosmic rhythms, and how they connect to the microcosm, to us as human beings. For instance, there is some evidence that where a breast cancer patient is in her monthly cycle could determine the outcome of her surgery.

"I came across this intriguing information in one of the medical journals I read in the library before my surgery," Erin confers. "That is why I scheduled my lumpectomy two weeks after my last period."

Scientists are also conducting studies on clinical depression, and how seasonal changes or even different times of the day might determine a person's condition. Even before science had a hand in anything, the yogis always knew that our own biorhythms are entrained by the cosmic rhythms.

"How do these cycles influence our lives?" Bryan asks.

The answer lies in what scientists call our circadian rhythm, or the pattern of biological cycles. Recurring at approximately twenty four-hour intervals, our body temperature fluctuations, hormone and enzyme production, electrolyte excretion and the sleep-dream-awake cycle all follow a rhythmic pattern.

I relate one of the first experiments proving the importance of circadian rhythms, which was conducted in Germany in 1968. A group of volunteers placed in a windowless room were systematically isolated from all external cues of time, like clocks, watches or calendars. The subjects were only allowed to establish and follow their own internal schedules for eating and sleeping—taking food only because of hunger, and laying down only when truly tired. What was revealed by this and subsequent studies was that our body seems to naturally operate on a cycle of approximately twenty-five hours, called the "free-run" period. Similar observations suggest that the rhythmic changes in our bodies are not only produced by an *outside* environment or lifestyle, but are based on an *internal* factor as well.

Our *inner body clock*--the mechanism that rouses us from sleep if our alarm clock fails to go off, and which reminds us to eat even when we are working way past the dinner hour—does tend to run slightly different from the *solar day*.

Exhibiting a one hour difference, our inner clock runs twenty-five hours instead of twenty-four. It is this discrepancy that gives "cir-cadian" its true meaning: from Latin, "circa" means "about" and "diem" means "day." If we were to construct an imaginary watch based on the natural rhythm, it would be correctly timed only on the first day. On the second day, it would run an hour late, the third day two hours late and so on. According to the cycle, it would only be useful again after about twenty-four days.

Mike, who was ruled by his hectic schedule for so long, found it difficult to reset his own natural rhythms. Well, if our internal clocks are not *reset* on a daily basis, we will drift further and further off course, on account of the inherent twenty-five hour "free run" period. If we allow this free-running rhythm to control us, we could be eating breakfast at midnight, and getting into bed at dawn in just two weeks!

As Mike should know, our present-day references are not half as natural. We, unlike plants and animals, are most independent of the natural environment, and rely on *artificial* cues to inform us of the change. We set our clocks and adjust our watches with the radio, television or other's clocks and watches. We of our advanced technology have mostly fallen out of phase with the natural, cosmic rhythms because of electric light and standardized time: flipping a switch and reading a digital clock is faster, easier and more practical these days than following the path of the sun or counting the phases of the moon.

But above and beyond any man-made apparatus that can tell time and mark change, these rhythms of nature will continue to exist and exert their force. The sun will still rise and set, and the tides still ebb and flow. We might be enticed by what an irregular lifestyle has to offer—working a night shift to earn extra money, dancing into the wee hours at the clubs, watching the late show—but our body will eventually pay the price for being *out of phase* with these natural cycles or rhythms.

"When I got into drugs, I never even knew what time it was," Andre confesses. "You start to measure time by your last fix."

With any lifestyle, there is a whole social structure associated with it. Included in this is the element of society that exists outside of normal or average time constraints, and live by their addictions or dependencies.

Young children live by their parent's timetable, and the days of prisoners are segmented by the criminal justice system. Others, like teachers, students, and nine-to-fivers, work by daylight, and still others like police on the night beat or overnight radio personalities are productive when most of us are sleeping. Then there are those like myself who are on-call twenty-four hours, and must make themselves available day and night.

For thousands of years, the yogis, with fewer worldly commitments, have lived lives that almost entirely echo the rhythms of Nature.

134

Living among the animals, the forests and the rivers, their only reference is the world around them. They adapt to *natural* rhythms, meditating with the dawning and setting of the sun, and retiring with the moonrise.

Many of us may find the idea of living by nature appealing, but wonder how to keep ourselves on track after the weekend. If we mostly regulate time during the week, then we certainly make up for it by enjoying fewer constraints over the weekend. We may not have as many necessary *obligations* on Saturday and Sunday, but our social lives are fuller. Since the body clock tends to slow down, we tend to sleep in longer after staying out late, which causes a slight delay. This common phenomenon emphasizes the interactions, which normally occur between our body clock , social commitments and time cues. It is what makes it difficult to go to sleep at a decent hour on Sunday night, and resume a normal routine on Monday.

No wonder we get the "Monday morning blues," because our body temporarily misses the relaxed time state of the weekend and is reluctant to come back to reality!

We may be *physiologically* equipped to follow a natural rhythm, but technology and lifestyle often makes it difficult, like overwhelming social engagements that interfere with regular mealtimes, and disturb our sleep. We are more apt to adhere to man-made rules than those of nature...but in this way, we become more susceptible to both physical and psychological problems, like insomnia or mood disorders.

We depend on our body clock, yet so many of us have no idea where to locate it or how to set it. Situated on the undersurface of the brain, the body clock is composed of two small groups of cells called the *suprachiasmatic nuclei*. They are part of the now-familiar *hypothalamus*, which controls body temperature, intake of food and water, hormone secretion and sex drive. The *nuclei* also reside close to the regions of the brain that control sleep and alertness, and exchange information with these areas. They rest above the *optic chiasm,* where the two optic nerves carrying visual information cross over each other on their way to the vision center of the brain. Here is where the sensations of light and darkness are processed, as are our internal time cues.

Interestingly, the location corresponds with the *ajna,* or *brow chakra* in the *subtle body,* the focal point of meditation.

The human mind is a creature of habit, and we are often enslaved by our bad habits more so than our good ones. When we habitually disregard the natural time cues, we alter our schedules for the worst, and find ourselves falling out of synchrony with the cosmic rhythms around us. How then can we learn to take more notice of time cues, so that they do not overwhelm us? What attempts can we make to minimize the adverse influence on our mealtimes, and sleep/awake cycle?

As a point of reference, I make sure that I awake at the same time *every single day*—including weekends—*regardless* of what time I go to bed. Learning to adhere to a regular routine for a majority of the time, we allow our body clock to *reset* itself.

Mike argues that he and his wife Debra attend so many business functions over the weekend that they seldom get in until two in the morning. As a result, they often sleep into the late hours of the morning.

Though it may sound painful to begin with, keeping a consistent sleep cycle becomes habitual, even second nature. We should never demand or force sudden change upon ourselves, and any alteration we make in our behavior or lifestyle should be made very gradually. Even awakening five to ten minutes earlier—until it becomes natural—is beneficial. In increments, we eventually may find ourselves able to rise at the peaceful hours between four and six a.m., or what the yogis revere as *brahmamuhurta*, or the "hour of the lord."

Now that we are awake, it is time to make the *first appointment* with ourselves and meditate. The transition in *awareness* provides the *melody* on a background of the constantly changing, celestial *rhythm*. Both the sleep/awake and the dark/light cycle are occurring simultaneously, making it an ideal moment for meditation. In this way, we are living in *harmony* with nature.

Now that they are married, but continue to work different schedules Nicole and Bryan show their concern about meal and sleeptimes.

After meditating, a light, nourishing breakfast eaten between six and eight a.m. is another healthy start to our day. The word "breakfast" literally means to "break a fast"; this refers to the *ideal* twelve to sixteen hour "fast" that occurs between the last meal taken the evening before, and our first meal of the morning.

With the sun at its height, there is peak activity in the *manipura*, or *solar chakra*, so lunch is best metabolized at noon. Contrary to our custom, lunch should be the heaviest meal of the day, though we often "save" calories for dinner, and often eat too much too close to bedtime. Though dinner is the most difficult meal to regulate—timewise, and in terms of quantity—it is ideal that we eat at sunset, and seldom two hours before retiring. Past this time, the fire element in the *solar chakra* is low, and late-night eating causes digestive problems.

After Erin underwent surgery, she had lost her appetite, and remembers seldom sleeping. Melatonin tea—touted as a sedative—helped her insomnia somewhat, but did not allay her anxieties.

Called the "darkness indicator" and "internal time cue," melatonin provides the link between the environment and our own body clock.

The nocturnal surge of melatonin—from sunset to sunrise—peaks at two a.m., as the hormone's release promotes restful sleep. Due to solar influence, hormone production ceases during the day, otherwise we would literally go to sleep every time we felt tired!

Cosmic Eye

Melatonin is the body's "natural wonder" drug, and is now considered an *anti-stress, anti-cancer* and *anti-aging* hormone. The hormone is actually produced by a small structure buried deep in the brain—the *pineal gland*. Since time immemorial, this tiny and mysterious gland has been regarded as the "seat of the soul." Located at the level of the *ajna chakra,* or the "third eye of man," the *pineal gland* is the focal point of meditation.

For many years, however, doctors considered it to serve no useful function. Needless to say, the "yoga view" was scoffed at. Only now has traditional medicine come to realize its secret power.

This master gland is the regulator of regulators. It is "photosensitive," as the polarized light of the moon and solar brightness affects pineal activity. This explains the relationship between phases of the moon, pineal activity, the menstrual cycle and mood disorders.

The gland is "thoughtsensitive"as well. It responds positively to things like music, aromatherapy, focusing, visualization and *mantras*. Negative thoughts, however, like anger, hate, greed, anxiety and depression negatively influence the gland's rhythmic activity and melatonin production. Several bi-polar disorders such as schizo-affective, or seasonal disorder, and manic-depressive illness, are associated with lack of melatonin. Suicide victims usually have low melatonin levels, as do schizophrenics, alcoholics and addicts. In fact, anti-depressant therapy unknowingly corrects the problems by utilizing serotonin to increase melatonin levels. Produced primarily by the *pineal gland,* serotonin is used to manufacture melatonin.

By its action on the thymus gland, melatonin strengthens the immune system. It reverses the immune impairment caused by psychological and physiological stress. Melatonin is thus an *anti-stress* hormone, and promotes restful sleep and relaxation.

By stimulating the immune system, melatonin slows the progression of AIDS. Andre, who has HIV positive status but has not exhibited any symptoms of AIDS, finds my comment very comforting.

"What about the *anti-cancer* element of melatonin?" Erin implores.

Disease simply means that certain cells or systems are not in resonance in the body's electromagnetic field. Nobel Prize winner Szent-Gyorgi believes that cancer is caused by a lack of bio-electronic resonance at the cellular level. Melatonin and DNA demonstrate bio-electric resonance, and thus maintain cellular health.

Many diseases, including cancer, have as their basis free radical damage. Melatonin is the most powerful anti-oxidant or free radical scavenger known to man. It therefore provides extensive *protection* to the cells and to the DNA from damage, and is then able to minimize the *potential* for disease, or cancer. Reestablishing the magnetic resonance, it creates harmony in the DNA.

Melatonin also has profound influence on the proper *timing* of the cell division. Low melatonin levels allow uncontrolled cell multiplication. Several scientists have found that a cause of cancer is low level of melatonin in the blood and a malfunctioning pineal gland. They found an improvement in health and increased remission as melatonin levels increased.

"Since it fights stress and disease, melatonin must determine how fast we age," Joe infers.

Joe has unknowingly revealed the "guarded secret," because being in phase with nature *is* the secret to longevity! When our body clock remains out of synchrony with the natural rhythm, it not only predisposes us to sleep, stress and disease, but also accelerates the aging process.

When the many "subordinate" clocks that help to run the body—respiratory, heart, reproductive and others—begin to lose their connection to the "master body clock" in the brain, aging occurs.

By delaying the onset of age-related diseases such as Parkinson's, Alzheimer's, heart disease, cancer and others, melatonin defers aging. A three billion year-old molecule found in all life forms within the evolutionary cycle, ranging from algae to humans, melatonin is essential to life. It plays a critical role in cell physiology, and determines how well and how long we live.

By targeting the thymus gland, melatonin produces T-lymphocytes and NK, or natural killer cells that are *anti-cancer* surveillance cells. Responsible for youthfulness and longevity, the thymus gland atrophies as we age...but there is compelling evidence that thymic aging is reversible! Researchers have found that melatonin may be the natural *anti-aging* hormone, which together with the pituitary and thymus glands, can slow down the aging process, and promote youthfulness and longevity.

"Are you recommending an over-the-counter melatonin supplement?" Bryan inquires.

Such supplemental melatonin is useful in treating insomnia, jet lag and regulating sleep cycles in blind individuals. But the magnitude of self-produced melatonin is far greater than taking it orally. The levels of natural melatonin are not only three to ten times greater, but also follow natural biorhythms, which *external*, artificial means can never duplicate. Therefore, for general long-term health, melatonin *must* be produced from *within* our "inner world."

The only way we can unveil this secret power is by focusing on this "thoughtsensitive" *brow chakra* in meditation. Like I always say, meditation *is* the best medication.

Scientists at the University of Massachusetts have found this association between meditation and increased melatonin levels with possible therapeutic implications specifically for breast and prostrate cancer. Meditation increases melatonin levels, thus preventing cancer and slowing down the aging process.

For Erin, meditation provides a new hope to maintain her breast cancer in remission besides relieving her chronic stress and insomnia.

I have also discovered that sleep and meditation go hand in hand. Because we are naturally transported to a more enlightened realm in deep sleep, the same sense of timelessness is cultivated in meditation.

In meditation, we transcend the mundane and the superficial as we learn to put time on hold. We are moved by our own breath, not by the hands of a clock, when we maintain the posture and "touch oblivion." This is when we are most likely to connect with the natural rhythm of time, as we are mostly distracted by artificial means in "everyday life."

Just imagine the synchronized sensation we feel in meditation continuing to effect us for the rest of the day...that is what happens when we become accustomed to our internal body clock.

Like the rhythms of life, the entire practice of yoga is dedicated to balance. We flow through the *sun salutations*, each movement melting into the next. The physical practice culminates in meditation and continues to realign our daily rhythm even after we step off the mat. The eurhythmics of yoga incorporate all the aspects of nature that are called upon to create balance on earth.

Chapter Sixteen

Mirror Image

Even as a falcon or an eagle, after soaring in the sky,
folds his wings for he is weary, and flies down to his nest,
even so the Spirit of man hastens to that place of rest
where the soul has no desires and the Spirit sees no dreams.
—from the Upanishads

Under the cover of moonlit sky, we will travel several journeys. Our voyage begins on the surface of the ocean, where the beam of the moon's reflection shimmers. Here we float with half of our body in the water, and the other half still in the air. The movement of the waves carries us, drifting wherever they want us to go. The moonlight dims and the current slows as we slip a little deeper to become immersed in the quieter waters below the surface.

Drowsiness, or the first stage of sleep, heralds this transition between the conscious and the unconscious. Here, the surface of the waking world is still within our reach, and we can be aroused quite easily. This is the light sleep we fall into while we lay in the sun at the beach: subliminally, we can still hear waves crashing, seagulls calling to each other and children playing in the sand right near us, though these sounds seem far away. Yet we suddenly awake if someone stands in the way of our sun, casting a shadow over us. So at this level, we are still able to sense what is happening in our environment and react to it.

As we sink further into unconscious, our temperature decreases and our breathing and heart rate slows down. Our entire body is now paralyzed, able to perform only the most vital functions as we progress to deep sleep. Sleep is a distinct state—the body is at rest, the metabolism lowers, and the mind becomes oblivious to the world outside. The *awareness* transcends the physical to enter the higher realms, and yet our *aliveness* continues to sustain the physical.

Though it does not become unconscious entirely, our mobile *awareness* shifts its *direction*. Each night, it journeys from the *physical* to the *subtle* to the *causal* plane, where it touches its destination— the domain of the Spirit. Before we awake, it returns once again to the physical realm, which has remained on "auto-pilot" during the excursion.

Enclosed in an undisturbed silence, we are momentarily disconnected from the world. We enter deep sleep each night and we return each morning without memory of where we have been. It is said by the great yoga masters to be more profound than the dream and awake states of consciousness.

During our excursions through the unconscious, we are carried through different depths of sleep a night. With one yielding softly into another, the stages of sleep evolve from an almost waking state of consciousness, to the deepest *delta* states. Research has shown that different states of consciousness generally produce corresponding brain wave patterns when recorded on an EEG. Our brainwaves are constantly changing, and they are classified as four separate stages in the course of the sleep cycle.

Beta waves (16 cycles per second) are a rapid and irregular pattern associated with usual waking consciousness. *Alpha* waves are slower and more rhythmic (10 cycles per second) and indicate a more tranquil mental state. The even *theta* waves (8 cycles per second) are associated with a state of reverie, and inner exploration. The lowest state of nervous system arousal equated with deep sleep is indicated on the EEG by the *delta* waves at only 0.5 to 4 cycles per second.

There are two basic kinds of sleep patterns that occur in regular and predictable cycles. The first sleep state is associated with dreaming and is identified by observation of REM, or rapid eye movements. When awakened from REM sleep, we are usually able to recall our dreams in vivid detail. This is not so in deep sleep, or the *delta* stage. Aroused out of such deep levels, we often find it hard to orient ourselves to the environment and are unable to report any dream activity.

Normally, sleep rotates in cyclic sequence, progressing from light to deeper stages and then again returning to lighter sleep. During a single night's sleep, this cycle is repeated four to five times. We move fairly quickly through the more active states, descend into deep sleep, and finally resurface to REM sleep once again. With each subsequent cycle, the period of deep sleep is a little shorter,

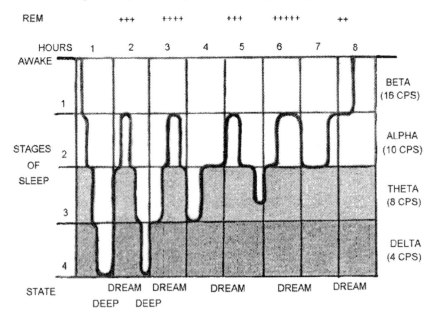

FIGURE 14. SLEEP CYCLES AND STAGES

and more time is spent in the dreaming state. After the first four or five hours, we have already profited from any amount of deep sleep that is allotted us each night. When we have the urge to sleep longer, what this really seems to indicate is a desire to dream more, not a need for more deep sleep. (Fig.14)

With this knowledge, it is interesting to consider that yoga advocates only four to five hours of sleep a night as sufficient. According to the philosophy, no human or animal "sleeps" for more than three-and-a-half hours, which obviously refers to the deep sleep state. Even research conducted in sleep laboratories validates the ancient belief—studies prove that any *additional* sleep is spent dreaming. The modern standard of sleep generally encompasses *both* dreaming and deep sleep, but yoga maintains that *wakefulness, sleeping* and *dreaming* are three distinct states.

It may seem that *quality* sleep happens all by itself. We know that when we wake up refreshed in the morning, with a pleasant sense of vitality that lasts throughout the day, we have had a good night's sleep.

In deep sleep, we breathe from the diaphragm, so it provides a fortitude against accumulated stress and fatigue as it activates our homeostatic, or balancing mechanisms—the tools of self-repair. After all, the purpose of the *delta* state is to rejuvenate the body, and revitalize the *prana*, or life force.

Progressive episodes of deep sleep occur for shorter and shorter periods as the night moves on, however, and we soon enter REM, or dream sleep. Our bodies remain still, but our minds become active again—even our eyes move as if we are scanning a page. Our brain is extremely active during the dream state, due to the great supply of blood flow.

If we are awakened suddenly, we can often vividly recall the "script" we were following or acting out as the dream progressed. Most of us have the urge to sleep longer when the alarm goes off, because what we really desire to do is return to the dream state. Our conscious mind becomes enticed by what has materialized in the unconscious, and it seeks closure—in other words, it wants to finish what it started.

Sigmund Freud theorized that dreams are conscious expressions of repressed, unconscious impulses and wishes. In dreams, these desires are distorted in such a way that the ego will find them acceptable. Psychologically speaking, our dreams become a sort of refuge. Within the confines of our established personalities, certain things can be rationalized, but other things seem grossly inappropriate and we would seldom conceivably go through with them.

If we are continually frustrated at work, we can often project our feelings while we dream. What happens in the dreaming state is that we live out our latent desires and any unfinished business of the day.

Joe, who often had fantasies about killing his boss, was not literally inclined to be a murderer. That is why we go off quietly into the night and satisfy our desires by escaping into a dream world. Here we are safe to gratify our impulses with abandon, though there is a good chance that we will still become emotionally involved. If we dream of something forbidden to us, like pursuing extramarital relationships or stealing company funds, we may wake up with a lingering sense of guilt as if we had truly taken the action.

Our mind has created a memory of having indulged a fantasy. From the dream, we know just how involved we were, and how pleasurable or gratifying it was, regardless of the consequences. So when the dream returns, the unconscious memory of the dream is even stronger and has to be dealt with again. The second or third time we have the dream, we add new material, which *reinforces* the memory of the dream even more. It is no wonder that we often wake up exhausted because such repetitive dreams deplete us of both mental and physical energy.

Dreaming is an issue of energy, after all. It does not teach us to concentrate or focus, but instead dissipates our resources. It is the subliminal impressions stored in the unconscious mind that produce dreams.

"I think I subconsciously collected everything I read or saw about cancer, and took it to bed with me," Erin tells me. "In my dreams, cancer was lurking behind every corner."

As a result, she eventually developed insomnia, since sleepless nights were preferable to her recurring nightmares. Likewise, the actions we perform while awake are also driven by unconscious desires. So much energy is tied up in expressing these desires that we act them out without realizing it, or we perpetrate them in dreams. Either way, that energy is not available for us to use consciously and constructively.

Nicole relates to nightmares in much the same way. In her dreams, she continually lost control of everything, and was completely paralyzed to change what was happening.

Like Erin's, Nicole's dreams were a direct projection of how helpless and out-of-control she felt. Reinforcing this was her dependency on the prescription she took everyday. Though Valium might have gotten her to fall asleep, it nevertheless compounded the problem by interfering with *quality* sleep.

A psychotropic substance like Valium, or an illegal narcotic such as heroin, induces drowsiness or even stupor, yet they interfere dramatically with the natural sleep cycle. Both are sedatives, but produce only a false sense of rest since they compromise deep restful sleep.

"On drugs, I was numb all the time," Andre relates. "I'd be nodding off for hours, and couldn't lift my head off the pillow, but can't ever remember feeling refreshed."

For others like Nicole and Andre, yoga and meditation are not only methods used to calm anxiety and face pain, but paths to follow in which to reclaim the many hours of deep sleep lost while under the influence of mind-altering substances.

Though both dreaming and meditation process unconscious material, we can differentiate between the two. Dreaming deals with unconscious desires, and adds fuel to the fire *without* contributing to our personal growth. Meditation is a dynamic method, and brings about an inner evolution in the mind by *dispensing* the unconscious material.

When we dream, we are swept away by our desires, reinforcing them and becoming entranced by our own *participation* in order to fulfill them. And while we may very well be confronted with the same longings in meditation, we simply *observe* them. We deal with them, but we do not strengthen or create more of them. Becoming aware of these impulses, and letting them drift by; we are now able to purge the *data banks* of our unconscious...that is the *difference* between meditation and dreaming.

Man has forever been fascinated by the mysteries of the dream world, and has indulged in unveiling its secrets. Those of pagan tradition in Nordic and Germanic lands believed that the sun in summer solstice provided access to unseen worlds like dreams. According to tradition, such followers would place sleep-inducing herbs like Valerian or St. John's Wort under their pillow to encourage dreams that could foretell the future. Midsummer is still a prominent holiday in Scandinavian regions, and a large part of the folklore centers on deciphering these prophetic dreams by experienced practitioners.

Today, many of us seek out a modern day equivalent—a psychiatrist, a psychoanalyst or even a fortune-teller— to help us make sense of our dreams. A more efficient way to analyze dreams—without a bill at the end of the month—is to engage in meditation!

Most people assume that only a qualified professional is able to analyze dreams. Although it was Freud who said that the purpose of dream analysis is to make the "unconscious conscious," it is really the yogi who guides the way toward accomplishing this goal in the most complete way.

In yoga philosophy, the role of the *delta*, deep sleep state has long been recognized as the time when consciousness can leave the dream levels and touch its very source—the domain of the Spirit.

Deep sleep is a timeless and wordless state, and the ego, or our "lower self"ceases to exist, enabling us to unite with the higher Self unbeknownst to us. After all, our waking consciousness is limited by the restrictions imposed by the ego-self.

Our ego-identification creates a pseudo-reality, and in turn, we lose touch with our core, or inner reality. Because of this, deep sleep is essential, since it returns us to this inner reality. By diving into our deepest recesses, into a splendid underwater kingdom to drink from an energizing fountain, we emerge anew, refreshed.

There is a fourth state called *turiya,* which is the ultimate dimension of higher *awareness*. To unite the deep sleep state with *awareness* is to reach *Samadhi*, or Enlightenment. Such a unity is a way of healing the "schizophrenic" existence we normally lead in everyday life. In sleep, we relinquish our "insanity" and are able to escape ourselves, returning to unity. After this brief flight to freedom, we usually awake to find ourselves entrapped again in the snares of daily life.

Though sleep is mostly taken for granted, millions of people continue to suffer from insomnia and sleep-deprivation. A common culprit of fragmented or disturbed sleep is an agitated mind. It seems that we do not really know how to get deep, restful sleep. Maybe because we have never regarded sleep as a skill!

Yogis are "professional sleepers," in that they can minimize and virtually eliminate the dream state. They regard deep sleep as the only stage essential for *prana* rejuvenation. Meditation is the first appointment they make with themselves, and deep sleep is the last and most important one of all. *Quality* sleep means *quality* meditation, and an overall state of well being throughout the day.

Mike admits that his wife Debra has been vicariously affected by his stressful lifestyle, and has been taking sleeping pills for awhile.

I assure him that a bad sleeper is not going to be made into a good sleeper by just a sleeping pill. Most of our sleep dilemmas are caused by poor sleep hygiene, in fact. If we go to bed stressed out, or at varying times of the night, if we eat, imbibe alcohol, or watch disturbing programs before we retire, we will unknowingly suffer the consequences the next day.

Deep Immersion

First and foremost, timing is everything. Ideally, we should go to sleep between 10 and 11 p.m. Our body starts to revert back to an active state after 10 p.m., so it then becomes more difficult to fall asleep. We are also more inclined to wake up early to meditate when we remain synchronized with natural rhythms.

After he was laid off, Joe developed the habit of staying up and watching late-night TV, since he found no reason to get up early.

Becoming addicted to prime time and late-night television, he believed that it actually helped him get to sleep. What we often forget is that by watching television, we invite visual images into bed with us. Many people believe that reading or listening to radio talk shows is another sleeping solution, but they are still being influenced. Stored in the subconscious, these images must be addressed, and eventually processed, in the dream state. Such processing prolongs the dream state, thus depleting our energy resources, and shortens the deep *delta* stage within the sleep cycle.

So if possible, we might want to videotape our favorite shows, and watch them at a more preferable time. When we have the urge to pick up a book when we can not sleep, it is best to resist. Even if we can not sleep, our body still benefits from lying down and being at rest. I find that soft music makes for a conducive sleeping environment, since it can entrain our internal rhythm to a more restful state.

We often awake to the *same* thoughts that we go to sleep with. If the last image we had was TV coverage of a plane wreck or a movie murder mystery, our nightmares may reflect what we have seen, and leave an "aftertaste" upon awakening. It is no wonder that most religions have followed the yoga dictum of saying a prayer or *mantra* before bedtime.

"The only solace I ever found from cancer was when I would sit down to pray before I tried to sleep," Erin confides. "It always seemed to fill me with new hope."

As our transiting *awareness* progresses toward the spirit, our affirmations become the passage to our journey into deep sleep.

"Instead of prayer, I resorted to alcohol as a sedative," Mike says. "Somehow, it had a way of making me feel worse."

"I would mix heroin with alcohol all the time," Andre adds. "Two downers seemed better than one."

Even though alcohol has been touted as a sedative, it deprives us of deep and restful sleep, and is often associated with sleep disorders like sleep apnea and narcolepsy. Alcohol does promote sleepiness, but it is only a false sense of rest. Under the influence of alcohol, we tend to dream more and compromise the time we spend in the deep *delta* levels. Studies indicate that alcohol abuse is more prevalent in chronic insomniacs than in the general population. What counters both alcoholism and substance abuse, and restores sleep in the process, is the powerful antidote of meditation.

Having a glass of wine with dinner early in the evening should not have too much of an adverse effect on our sleep.

Eating too close to bedtime, particularly a heavy meal with caffeinated beverages, imposes additional demands on our systems, which has to shut down during sleep. Caffeine in general should be avoided at any time later than 6 or 7 p.m. A four-hour time interval between our last meal, and when we go to bed is the healthy choice.

Energy is also diverted from the digestive process when we engage in vigorous exercise before retiring. Although it is good for us at any other time, it disturbs the metabolism, and does not allow for proper digestion, at night. Mostly low impact activity, like a stroll or slow dancing, usually will not interfere too much.

We can learn to remedy these problems with a little discipline. We can overcome insomnia, improper digestion and substance dependencies by learning to regulate our sleep hygiene.

In their own discipline of *yoga nidra*, the yogis capitalize on their control of the breath and access to the *autonomic nervous system*—their "inner world." Taking a cue from the masters, we lie in *shavasana*, or corpse posture, and begin counting the breath, with each exhalation twice as long as the inhalation. This breathing must be even and diaphragmatic, from the nose. Placing our hands on the abdomen, we are better able to feel the rising and falling of each inhale and exhale.

152

It is best to maintain a comfort level of a 1:2 ratio of breathing without pause or hesitation. Easily attained is a count between 4:8 or 3:6. Reducing *sympathetic arousal* during inhalation, we influence the *autonomic nervous system* to our advantage. Extending the exhalation—by stimulating the *parasympathetic arm*—induces further relaxation.

The exercise itself describes taking eight full breaths lying on our back, and then sixteen breaths lying on our right side and finally, thirty-two breaths on our left side. If we are not asleep after our first attempt, we can repeat the exercise as needed. Like any new skill we learn, it must be practiced consistently. We only find it useful when it helps us fall asleep and stay asleep.

What most people never realize is that sleep is a skill that requires *concentration*. Sleep only happens when we first *negate* the environment around us—the room, the bed and the blanket—and finally, our own bodies. Once here, we concentrate on darkness and silence, or the "negative." Meditation is somewhat similar, in that it is also a withdrawal from "all spaces and places," but here the focus is on inner illumination, or the "positive."

Since our mind field converges to a *quintessence* every time we sink into deep sleep or meditate, it is suggested that we fix our mind on the memory of "intoxication" of deep sleep, and preferably meditate immediately after such an experience.

The true knowledge of sleep thus derived enhances meditation. When the mind becomes stabilized—by absorbing this conscious experience –we understand this correlation better. In that, one echoes the other, meditation is perceived as the "mirror image" of deep sleep. Knowing, however, that the pure Self is *ever-awake* and that *only* the conscious part of the mind actually sleeps, we can observe the sleep process by dwelling in it. The higher mind will then observe the lower, sleeping mind, entering *yoga-nidra*, or conscious sleep.

The yogis have long utilized this wisdom for enlightenment. They transported the *unaware* but intoxicating and euphoric experience of deep sleep, to the *aware* experience in deep meditation. For the yogi, this total *adsorption* of *awareness* was heightened *enstacy*, or *Samadhi*.

Even though we touch the inner Self *transiently* in deep sleep, we usually remain unaware of the experience. Meditation helps us uncover the mysterious nature of deep sleep, and when we discover it for ourselves, like the eagle after soaring in the sky, we fold our wings and descend to that place of rest within ourselves.

Chapter Seventeen

Fire of Life

To keep gluttony at bay, leave on the tray
a quarter of the food served to you:
in this way, you will make progress
in your journey toward yoga.
—Yoga Darshana Upanishad

The ancient yogis have said that "One must eat in proper measure, and the proper measure of food is determined by the strength of one's gastric fire." Within the realm of the *manipura chakra*, or at the solar plexus, is located the digestive oven; according to the masters, the man who has achieved self-control fuels his "gastric fire" with only wholesome food and drink, and eats only when he is truly hungry. This heat energy regulates our digestive process. And when it comes to eating, our lack of self-control invites in a host of physiological problems.

We have all been told "You are what you eat" by someone, sometime in our life.

What we have learned from this deceptively simple phrase is that food not only affects the body, but determines the mind-set as well. There exists a continuous interplay between the two, though we still underestimate the power of proper nutrition. The yogis knew this, and have always stressed that the mind affects the diet, as the diet affects the mind.

155

If our mind is disturbed, we can miss the subtle cues that tell us when to eat and what food is appropriate to eat. If we are irritable and feel fragmented, our eating habits are more likely to be erratic. For instance, "midnight cravings," snacking in-between meals or choosing improper foods become habitual, and if we continue to indulge our bad habits, digestive problems will undoubtedly ensue.

Emotional and psychological factors share a direct connection to the digestive system. Often, what we choose to eat stems from our conditioned behavior. Our tendency to select stimulants like sugar and caffeine reflects our need to be instantly satiated, conditioned as we are by our fast-paced, contemporary lifestyle.

Bryan usually starts his day by gulping coffee and a cheese danish, in a rush to get to the office. Like Bryan, most of us remain unaware of the relationship between our restlessness, irritability, tiredness and our habitual use of sugar and caffeine.

Sugar and caffeine are the most obvious of the quick "energy fixes" to which we resort. Following the initial rush or euphoria is weakness, exhaustion or a hunger more intense than before. And the more we crave sugar and/or caffeine, the more dependent we become, and this is what I refer to as a "fatal attraction."

Caffeine depletes our energy stores without replenishing them. The "boost" after a cup of coffee is short-lived, leaving us even more fatigued and reaching for another cup. Likewise, a sugar "fix" contributes to an immediate rise in blood sugar levels and encourages an abrupt, untimed release of insulin. This in turn leads to relative *hypoglycemia,* or low blood sugar, which makes us irritable or withdrawn. Our mood then interferes with proper digestion.

Like our food choice influences our moods, our moods in turn affects digestion of the foods. Stress, adding fuel to the "gastric fire," is reflected in the stomach's increased acid secretion and can burn a hole—or an ulcer—in the lining. This often leads to constant snacking to keep the fire "extinguished."

Even after his two angioplasties, Joe still had chest pains and heartburn, which were undoubtedly a result of his stressful job situation. And as well as a heart condition, he was also diagnosed with an ulcer.

On the other hand, the hopeless, helpless feeling of depression causes inadequate acid secretion, setting the digestive oven on low heat. When the stomach decreases its acid output, protein digestion is impaired. Consequently, the mucous layer, a major protective barrier against bacteria in the lining of the small intestine breaks down, encouraging bacterial overgrowth. This results in unpleasant indigestion and flatulence.

Some psychiatrists even contend that a primary cause of depression may be liver dysfunction. Although the organ is often not thought of in this way, the liver provides another strategic link between nutrition and the mind. In addition to being a metabolizer of *emotions*, scientists have actually counted over 500 functions of the liver!

All the nutrients coming from the intestinal tract—with the exception of a large proportion of fats—go directly to the liver, the body's chemical factory. It is here that the nutrients are processed and released into the bloodstream, and the wastes, contaminants and toxins that build up in the body are filtered out.

As in the case of liver failure, toxic products accumulate in the bloodstream, interfering with the level of *awareness*. Commonly seen in severe hepatic dysfunction is a patient's fluctuation of consciousness, ranging from drowsiness, lethargy and stupor, to coma.

The liver must work many times harder if we consistently overeat, or overindulge in alcohol.

"I took my last drink six months ago, around the time I started meditating," Mike explains. "Drinking was an escape, but it made me hostile. Eliminating alcohol made me want to eat healthy and slow down."

Alcohol and foods extremely high in animal protein or fat content require increased excretion on the part of the liver. Because of excessive alcohol and poor food quality, the liver's capacity to modulate and provide an even flow of energy gradually weakens over time. This generates mental sloth and inertia, which in turn perpetrates our unhealthy eating and drinking habits so we become caught in a vicious cycle.

When the liver weakens, the body's compensatory organs, like the adrenal and thyroid gland, are unnecessarily activated and further aggravate stress, chronic tension and anxiety. Until the wastes are cleared from the blood, there will be a lack of clarity in the mind. It is no wonder that when we squelch the digestive flame, we are plagued with problems.

Meal Time

First and foremost, eating at regular intervals not only insures proper digestion, but gives us a sense of mental clarity and balance. During digestion, blood is diverted away from the brain, and our ability to think clearly is somewhat impaired. Eating at irregular times and in-between meals inconsistently and constantly stimulates the entire digestive process. Either way, we find it difficult to be productive.

Since there is a natural tendency to rest while we metabolize our food, improper digestion occurs if our body is engaged in activity at this time. For example, *time-urgency*—as Mike so often experienced—encourages "eating on the run" which is as unsatisfying as it is unhealthy.

When there is a cooperative effort between the mind and body, we become sensitive to our subtle internal cues. Keeping up with the body clock and cosmic rhythms, the ideal meal times are at sunrise for breakfast, around noon for lunch and at sunset for dinner. Eating three balanced and properly timed meals a day is the yoga discipline. By following the cues that help guide us into making proper food choices at the appropriate times, we can overcome our urge to eat at irregular intervals or to "grab a bite."

Thanksgiving

To allow good digestion, we should preferably eat in congenial company or in the pleasant silence of solitude. Once we are in a restful, comfortable state, we may then give thanks for what we are about to eat—in the form of a silent or vocal prayer, affirmation or *mantra*. This prepares both the mind and body to take nourishment. After all, food in itself is an offering from Nature, as is the act of eating a form of worship.

By saying "grace" before a meal, we focus our *awareness* and become more mindful of with what we are offering our "temple."

Elixir of Life

Ideally, it is best to take nothing more than water *before* and *after* we eat, since quenching the thirst during a meal dilutes the digestive juices, squelching the digestive flame.

About 2,000 chemical additives are used daily to make food and beverages look and taste appealing to the general public. On average, we eat between an estimated three to five pounds of these additives a year. Colored, carbonated and caffeinated beverages contain additives and chemicals that the body does not need, so water is the preferred choice.

Cool water is better than iced or cold, which shocks the system and can inhibit digestion. For a healthy individual, drinking six to eight glasses of water a day helps flush out the system and eliminates toxins. It also restores the fluids lost by sweating, exercise and elimination. Caution should be exercised, however, in those individuals with certain conditions that cause fluid retention.

Savor the Flavor

Not only do we readily consume unwanted chemicals and preservatives, but we ingest them so hurriedly that we compromise our digestive process. Unbeknownst, one third of digestion takes place in the mouth, where food must first be broken down and swallowed.

Like I always say, "chew the liquids and drink the solids." Solid food has to be first be *dissolved* in saliva on the tongue before it can be tasted. Incomplete chewing not only accounts for improper digestion, but also allows us to overeat, since we are almost literally "swallowing our food whole."

Studies done on obese people cite that once they develop the habit of chewing their food slowly, they eat much less. By savoring the flavor of each bite, we become satiated earlier, keeping gluttony at bay.

Nature's Choice

Living in harmony with nature, the yogis defined the inherent vegetarian nature of man by observing the eating and drinking habits of animals. They noted that those who ate only with a vertical movement of the jaw, and who took water with their tongues were inherently carnivorous. For example, the tiger brings its sharp incisors to use while tearing raw meat. In contrast, the cow uses both horizontal and vertical jaw movement to munch grass or weeds, and also drinks with its lips. Likewise, we drink in the same way, and our own jaw movement is bi-directional.

160

Apparently, grains, vegetables and fruit are Nature's offering that is most fit for human—or herbivore—consumption. We consume far more sufficient calories and nutrition by eating grain directly—as a primary consumer—than by obtaining it through grain fed beef.

And it is encouraging that people—my patients included—are beginning to eat more vegetables, fruits, grains and legumes, and less animal protein. But meat consumption in this country is still too high, even when there is growing evidence that it increases the incidence of cancer, heart disease and high cholesterol.

It is also well documented that a vegetarian lifestyle lowers blood pressure, and vegetarians seem to be less susceptible to osteoporosis than their meat-eating counterparts. Improvement in diet—mainly by reducing meat and increasing vegetable consumption—could prevent up to 40% of all worlds' cancer, according to a massive analysis of 4500 studies by the American Institute for Cancer Research and the World Cancer Research Fund.

It even takes 3.25 acres of agricultural land a year to feed an average meat eater. In contrast, a vegetarian needs only a half an acre. And more than 4,000 gallons of water are needed to produce one day's worth of food for a typical meat eater, whereas 1,200 is sufficient for a vegetarian.

Vegetarianism indirectly helps alleviate social and economic ills. To fatten livestock for consumption, they are fed tons and tons of grain a year. Just imagine how many starving families in impoverished countries we could feed with that amount!

While man has the reasoning power and can make intelligent food choices, animals eat indiscriminately. They eat whatever is available, even other animal and plant life laden with chemicals. The insecticides are then trapped in their own systems, with a concentration approaching one hundred times the original amount. Man is then subjected to the contaminated animal product when he makes meat part of his meal. Meat, poultry and fish contain two and one-half times more pesticides than most dairy products, and thirteen times the amount found in grains and vegetables.

Even in the most technologically advanced countries, additional contamination occurs while raising, packing and marketing meat products. When bred for consumption, animals are fed high-concentrations of estrogen hormones for weight gain and rapid growth. The ingestion of these hormones has been linked to breast cancer, fibroid tumors, menstrual irregularities and impotence in men.

"I recall my mother making meat the main course at every meal," Erin relates. "But after my lumpectomy, I realized the benefits of converting to vegetarianism."

Tons of antibiotics are also added to the feed of livestock yearly to keep the animals from falling ill. Animals raised in this fashion are far from healthy. Some develop malignant tumors, which are removed before packaging; these often escape food inspections and are sold alongside the prime cuts. To my knowledge, cancer in plants and vegetables is a non-issue. Unlike meat, rotten fruits and vegetables are easy to identify, and are thus discarded.

Meat has a natural tendency to deteriorate, which causes significant hygienic problems. When not destroyed by cooking, bacteria-laden meat leads to serious gastro-intestinal illnesses, including food poisoning. Over forty percent of hotdogs have more than enough bacteria growing in them to be considered "spoiled" by accepted standards.

Unlike its animal counterpart, vegetable protein seems to protect against the hardening of the arteries. In a study of Seventh Day Adventist vegetarians, those who ate no meat whatsoever had lower rates of cancer and heart disease than those who ate the same amount of meat as the average American.

162

Vegetarians also seem to have a larger intake of fiber in their diet. Besides decreasing arteriosclerosis (hardening of the arteries) and diverticulosis (weaknesses in the colon wall), vegetable fiber helps to eliminate environmental pollutants by absorbing them. With environmentalism on the rise, it is no wonder than that the vegetarian lifestyle is part of the growing health trend.

Two or three decades ago, a mere 1% of Americans claimed to be vegetarians. Today, about 10% of the American population—or 20 million people—say they are. Meatless products are sold at most fast food restaurants, and on airplanes, vegetarian meals continue to be the most commonly requested special meals.

"That is heartening to know, since I've mostly followed a vegetarian lifestyle," Nicole agrees.

Where's The Beef?

"But how can such a diet provide any protein?" Bryan asks. "And if we stop eating meat, how will we ever build muscle or get enough iron?"

As far as protein is concerned, those of us who wonder if a vegetarian diet is sufficient enough need not worry. In a comparison study of two hundred subjects—some on a meat-free diet and the others on a regular regime—neither group showed evidence of protein deficiency. As long as some dairy products were included in the diet, the intake of all nutrients was equal to or even greater than the recommended daily dietary allowances set by the National Research Council.

The medical and nutritional journals of today echo what ancient yogis said thousands of years ago—both proclaim that a balanced vegetarian diet is wholesome and healthful. (Fig.15)

Actually, protein is more a building block than a source of energy,

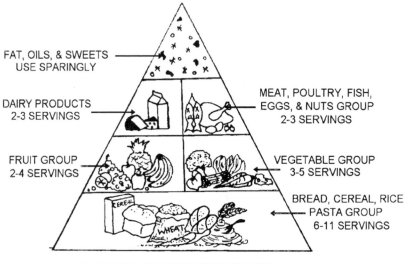

FAT, OILS, & SWEETS
USE SPARINGLY

DAIRY PRODUCTS
2-3 SERVINGS

MEAT, POULTRY, FISH,
EGGS, & NUTS GROUP
2-3 SERVINGS

FRUIT GROUP
2-4 SERVINGS

VEGETABLE GROUP
3-5 SERVINGS

BREAD, CEREAL, RICE
PASTA GROUP
6-11 SERVINGS

U.S. DEPT. OF AGRICULTURE 'S GUIDE

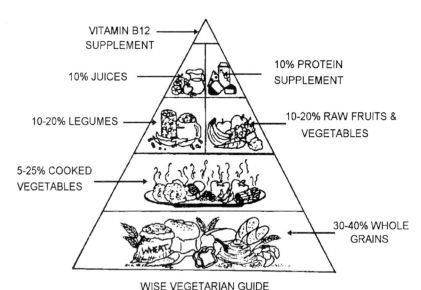

VITAMIN B12
SUPPLEMENT

10% JUICES

10% PROTEIN
SUPPLEMENT

10-20% LEGUMES

10-20% RAW FRUITS &
VEGETABLES

5-25% COOKED
VEGETABLES

30-40% WHOLE
GRAINS

WISE VEGETARIAN GUIDE

FIGURE 15. DAILY FOOD CHOICES

for it develops the framework of the bones, skin, cell walls, organs, blood vessels and muscles. During childhood and puberty, more protein is needed for growth and development. As we mature, we only require a daily allowance of protein for maintenance.

So if protein is essential for growth, development and maintenance, and we often seem to have a natural inclination to eat protein-rich foods like meat, why the advocation of the vegetarian lifestyle?

Fireplace

I consider proteins as the bricks we use to build a fireplace. We cement them into place to form the basic structure, and they are essentially what holds the fireplace together. They are an architectural necessity; without the framework to contain the flames, how would we safely and conveniently start the fire? However, we would never use them as the fuel itself because they are too solid: they would require extreme heat and leave excessive residue.

In our own body, animal protein is not a "clean burning fuel" since nitrogen atoms in meat can not be properly oxidized. For instance, six ounces of steak takes the stomach and intestines hours longer to digest than it would a serving of pasta the same size.

The nitrogen found in the amino acid molecules of animal products is harder to digest and the resulting production of urea and uric acid in the system overtaxes the kidneys, particularly the function of excretion. What can not be excreted or eliminated by the body accumulates in the tissues and joints, and the bodily environment soon becomes toxic. Such "protein toxicity" is responsible for conditions like gout and perhaps many degenerative illnesses. If we eat more protein than is necessary—especially if our carbohydrate intake is low—our body will begin to burn the protein like carbohydrate fuel, causing toxicity.

There is more than enough proof that a vegetarian diet provides more than enough protein. Nutritionists found that a 2,500-calorie diet would supply fifty percent more protein than is required by 98% of the population. The Recommended Daily Allowance of protein for women is 44 grams; the average vegetarian female consumes 65 grams. For men, it is 56 grams of protein; the average vegetarian male consumes 105 grams.

Interestingly, though protein is the "stuff of life," our bodies do not naturally produce it. Since we can not manufacture it, we must find protein in the environment that replenishes our stores. Furthermore, we do not accumulate stores of protein, like we do with carbohydrates and fats. Perhaps this explains why man covets high-protein foods like beef. Even our language reflects this idea that is so deeply rooted in our culture: after all, when we are referring to the very essence of something, we speak about the "meat" of the matter.

A Matter of Fat

Most cuts of meat contain nearly as much fat as they do protein. Even when the fatty parts are removed from the meat—like the "leaner" supermarket variety—it still contributes too much fat to our diet.

Bryan admits that even choosing lean meat over high-fat varieties has kept his cholesterol above 240.

Individuals on a low-cholesterol diet are also advised to generally avoid butter as well as meat. But unlike animal fat, butter is comprised of water and milk solids, which are water-soluble. The fat in butter differs from other saturated fats because of its surprisingly small chain length. Thus it does not have the same negative effect on the arterial lining as other animal fats. Butter softens when left out of the refrigerator, but beef will harden. It is no wonder that animal fats are known offenders for clogging the arteries.

Highly saturated fats, like animal fat, or lard, are *solid* at body temperature, while unsaturated vegetable fats are *liquid*. Most animals tend to store their energy in saturated fat chains, while plants store their own in unsaturated fat chains.

166

The length of the carbon chains that make up fats may vary widely. In butter, they range from four to eighteen carbons; in beef, fourteen to eighteen carbons. Longer chains tend to be more solid at body temperature, while shorter ones are more liquid.

For five centuries, *ghee*, or clarified butter, has been the best source of fat for human consumption when the watery part is removed so that only the clear fat is used. It not only makes foods more nutritious, but is an important ingredient in *Ayurvedic medicine*. It is also an excellent cooking fat, far superior to butter.

Margarine, long-touted as a healthier alternative to butter, is essentially a synthetic food. Interestingly, the incidence of heart attacks is higher in regions where margarine consumption is highest in relation to the general population who consumes butter. Artificially hydrogenated vegetable fats are a recent addition to the diet of man, and since our bodies have no previous experience with them, it seems reasonable to wonder if they have the capacity to break them down in the first place.

Vegetable oils have received even better press than butter, given their reputation for lowering cholesterol levels and preventing heart attacks. Polyunsaturated fatty acids have almost become virtually synonymous with heart protection in both popular and orthodox medical circles.

For centuries, Greeks and Italians have traditionally followed a diet that emphasizes lots of grains, fruits and vegetables, and replaces olive oil for butter and seafood for meat in most dishes.

Some dieticians recommend the Mediterranean diet over the original U.S. Food Guide Pyramid because it seems to provide better nutrition and quality of life. Many studies have documented the diet-related longevity of several groups of Italians, and have also observed that the inhabitants of the Greek Island, Crete, had one-twentieth the American death rate from heart disease.

The Japanese boast the world's lowest rate of heart disease overall, and the Chinese are only one-third as likely to develop colon cancer as Americans are, because the fat content in authentic Chinese and Japanese cuisine are among the lowest in the world—many dishes are only 15 to 20 percent fat, compared with 35 to 40 percent in the American diet.

In contrast, Americans suffer more diet-related illness since the average diet is composed of too much fat and too many "empty calories" like sugar. We are especially enticed by sweet foods, because they more often than not contain excessive amounts of both sugar and fat! Surprisingly, there are even "hidden" sugars in foods we would never suspect as being sweet—packaged meat products can contain nearly three percent of their weight in added sugar, and processed vegetables contain almost fifteen percent of added sucrose.

Adam's Apple

Just as Adam and Eve were unable to resist the temptation of the infamous apple, and mythological Hercules went in search of one covered in gold, man's natural affinity for sweets stems from an early desire to covet sugar. In Greek mythology, nectar—the sweetish liquid of flowers and fruit used by bees to manufacture honey—was even known as the "drink of the Gods."

Man himself began to cultivate sugar cane, and soon the process of refining sugar became industrialized, making sugar more widely available. As a result, the consumption of sugar has increased about eight times since the 1800's. Today, the average person eats about one hundred and twenty pounds a year! In fact, most of us eat our weight in sugar each year at the equivalent to one teaspoon of sugar an hour!

While sweets like dried fruits and honey contain large amounts of sugar, there is a larger percentage of fructose. Unlike sucrose, fructose is absorbed more slowly and does not trigger an insulin response.

Complex carbohydrates, as in whole grains, potatoes and the bulk of fruits and vegetables, sustain our energy for longer periods of time. The advantage of eating whole-grain cereal over a doughnut is obvious. Complex carbohydrates or starches are broken down slowly, unlike simple sugars that are absorbed immediately, giving us a quick "sugar high."

Those who experience drastic fluctuations in their blood sugar levels release more stress hormones like adrenaline, as seen in the "fight or flight" response. Over time, this leads to chronic stress, resulting in headaches, anxiety and fatigue.

"Maybe my stress is related to my own sugar highs and lows," Nicole adds. "When I'm nervous, the first thing I reach for is chocolate, without even realizing it."

"I preferred the brown sugar high myself," Andre says, jokingly.

By inculcating dietary *awareness*, both Nicole and Andre found that their addictions and cravings gradually diminished.

Nuts and Bolts

The body manufactures its own enzymes, and needs the essential vitamins and minerals in order to do so. Chemical "scissors" like enzymes are responsible for digesting food; they "cut" or break down large molecules into simpler units for energy release.

Unfortunately, in an average diet—consisting of meat and processed foods—the vitamin and mineral intake is suboptimal. The healthiest way to obtain vitamins and minerals is through food, but if the diet is deficient, supplements are in order.

If a large part of our diet is lacking in the essentials, then all the other foods we eat must make up for our nutritional needs. But on average, we are more apt to choose preserved fruits and vegetables over fresh, and processed or refined grains instead of whole. Such deficiencies add to our malnutrition.

Poverty amidst Plenty

A popular American meal consists of a hamburger, French fries and a soft drink. Such a diet contains the major ingredients of most poor quality foods: saturated fat, excess sodium and simple sugars. Other ready-prepared favorites, like packaged crackers or cookies, also contain additives and preservatives in the form of artificial flavorings, colorings and sweeteners.

Given our preference for junk food, it is really no wonder that two leading causes of death—heart disease and cancer—are at least partly related to dietary habits. And in spite of the growing trend toward health and fitness, the typical diet still consists of more fast food and less food from nature. It is estimated that Americans consume over fifteen billion hot dogs a year—if these were lined up end to end, they would probably extend to the sun and back!

It is a disheartening situation, but we do possess the power to extricate ourselves from it. We know that there are other world cultures that are more untouched by the types of cancer and coronary artery disease that are our number one killers.

Food for Thought

Through their knowledge of *prana*, the yogis defer entropy and enjoy longevity. From them, we can add years to our own lifespan by learning dietary *awareness*.

Everything that keeps the microcosm alive is the *prana,* which is derived from the essential sources. One of the most important ways we acquire *prana* from the macrocosm—besides the breath—is through food and water. *Prana,* which forms the essence of the mind and links it to the body, has to be constantly replenished. Food is one component of this dynamic energy, and without it our *aliveness* is subject to entropy.

When our dietary discipline is healthy, energy flow (*prana*) from the solar plexus, or *manipura chakra,* infuses us with vitality and an overall sense of well being. Both proper digestion and elimination help us to maintain a sense of equanimity, and a relaxed state of mind.

For both physical and mental vitality, we can choose to "eat in proper measure" by fanning the "gastric fire" with proper fuel. To overcome our increasing nutritional debt, we follow the path of the yogi. Their recipe for longevity includes wholesome and fresh foods like milk, yogurt, fresh vegetables, fruits, grains and legumes. Gradually eliminating our intake of refined sugar, processed foods and meat, and inculcating a vegetarian lifestyle helps us maintain a naturally healthy state.

The most basic and integral aspect of yoga and meditation is *ahimsa,* or non-violence in our speech, thought and action. Respect for all living things not only helps to preserve the ecological balance of life on our planet, but also protects against the "pollution" of our "inner world."

What we throw in our "gastric fire" will determine the kind of "smoke" emanating. Although fire burns rubber and incenses the same exact way, the smoke from one is black and noxious, and from the other it is pleasantly intoxicating. Similarly, what we ingest determines our mindset...for the essence of mind emanates from what we eat.

Chapter Eighteen

Body Language

The body is like a chariot
of which the soul is the owner;
the intelligence is its driver,
the mind plays the part of the reins;
as for the horses, those are the senses;
the world is their arena.
—Katha Upanishad

As a teenager, B.K.S. Iyenger—author of *Light on Yoga* and revolutionary teacher of *hatha* yoga—suffered from influenza, tuberculosis, malaria and typhoid fever. Stricken by poverty and disease for most of his young life, Iyengar was told that he was not made for yoga. His body—likened to "dry wood"—was not able to bend or stretch, and his breathing rate—at 30 to 35 breaths per minute—made *pranayama* impossible. Inspired nonetheless, he became his own instructor, consciously and consistently devoting himself to daily practice. Achieving mastery over his own physical and mental condition, he soon began teaching others.

At age 79, Iyengar continues to be one of the world's most influential yogis. Providing physical and mental strength and flexibility, regular *hatha* yoga practice teaches us to sustain deep concentration—the "secret ingredient" to Iyengar's recipe of self-mastery and progression.

Hatha yoga not only keeps us healthier, stronger, more coordinated and younger-looking, but increases our concentrative powers and expands our inner *awareness*. Incorporating both body and mind, it acts as a physical stimulant for the neural and glandular systems, reduces muscular tension and cleanses the body of accumulated toxins and wastes.

The practice of yoga builds a powerful body and a mind of equal stature, since physical equilibrium ensures emotional harmony, and vice versa. Once this is achieved, disease — literally, "dis-ease" —is all but eliminated.

Along with a healthy diet, exercise is our best defense against illness and the discomforts usually associated with the process of aging. Exercise also prevents cancers of the colon, breast and female reproductive tract, stroke, type II diabetes, hypertension and osteoporosis. Regular exercisers are less likely to put on extra weight, and become anxious or depressed.

A twenty-two year analysis of longshoremen in San Francisco demonstrated that vigorous physical labor significantly reduces the risk of heart disease, the leading cause of death in the United States. But despite the benefits of keeping active, only 22 percent of Americans get the recommended amount of exercise. As our world becomes more high-tech, fewer and fewer people cite manual labor as part of their job description. Now only 1 percent of us work at jobs that require any kind of physical labor. During the Industrial Revolution, human labor accounted for 30 percent of all occupations.

Is it really any wonder that we have become such an immobile nation when most of our jobs involve sitting at a desk for hours at a time? Another reason for our national inertia is the invention of remote control. To operate anything from a garage door to a TV to a CD player, we simply press a button. As a result, nearly 12 percent of all deaths—or 250,000 yearly—in this country are attributed to a sedentary lifestyle.

Since most work today—with the exception of professional athletes and dancers—no longer requires physical exertion, we have made exercise recreational, something to engage in on our own time. Many of us complain, however, that we do not have enough time in the day or week to exercise, yet—for the average viewer, at least—about one-third of the twenty-four hour period is spent watching television.

It is not time itself, but our *time management* that needs adjusting. Even if we devote just half the time we spend surfing the channels to exercise instead, we instantly decrease our risk of developing health problems.

One of the first studies to document the positive effects of even moderate exercise took place in London. Conductors who operated double-decker buses were 54 percent less likely to die from heart disease than bus drivers of the same age who were not required to walk up and down a flight of stairs every day. The same experiment found that postal delivery workers had healthier hearts than the more sedentary postal clerks did.

The investigators also monitored the effects of leisure-time exercise on a large group of white-collar workers over a period of nine years. Those who spent most of their free time being physically active only had a 3.1 percent chance of developing heart attacks, compared to 6.9 percent of those who did not exercise. In this particular study, none of these differences were ever explained by other factors such as smoking habits, existing hypertension, family history or obesity. Keeping active modifies the risk of coronary artery disease, one of the leading causes of death, and its associated conditions: high cholesterol and blood pressure, glucose intolerance, obesity and stress.

Physicians recommend exercising at least three times a week, at a minimum of 20 minutes of continuous aerobic activity. Keeping generally active for 30 minutes, five times a week, is an equally beneficial alternative. Even being active at different intervals throughout the day has a cumulative effect. It is estimated that incorporating any activity into our occupations—even climbing the stairs in lieu of the elevator, or using our break time to take a short walk—improves health in general, and may reduce the risk of future heart problems by as much as 49 percent.

But the success of any fitness program also depends on the *type* and *intensity* of the exercise. Divided into *isometric* and *isotonic* work, exercise is categorized according to the kind of muscular activity involved.

Isometric, or static exercise includes lifting weights or working out against any fixed resistance, like the exercise apparatus in the gym. Though we do not cover much distance in such a workout, substantial energy is expended. *Isometric* activity is bound to increase muscle strength or even bulk. The heart has to work against the weight or resistance, there is a rise in blood pressure, with relatively little increase in cardiac conditioning.

Our body becomes fatigued after such activity because we are creating tension in the muscle. Lifting weights shortens muscle fiber, and by increasing muscle tension, induces stress. Ideally, it should *only* be utilized to rebuild muscle tone and bulk during rehabilitation of musculoskeletal injuries. Since *isometric* work places a "pressure load" on the heart, it can be hazardous to patients with heart disease and high blood pressure.

In contrast, *isotonic*, or dynamic exercise like aerobics, bicycling, running or swimming enhances endurance, and produces adaptive and conditioning cardiovascular benefits in both athletes and patients. More than half of patients on antihypertensive medication are able to lower their dosage or discontinue use altogether when they start to follow an aerobic exercise program.

Since *isotonic* work imposes a "volume load," the heart accommo-

175

dates a greater volume of blood with each heartbeat which improves cardiac efficiency. Not only does *isotonic* work decrease heart rate and reduce blood pressure, but also raises our metabolism, so that we burn calories more efficiently.

Whether we engage in moderate or strenuous exercise, a remarkable physiological transition occurs. The body releases endorphins, or natural "pain killers" that produce what is called a "runner's high." The psychological effects of aerobic exercise are many—it reduces anxiety, tension and the tendency toward depression, and makes us more adaptable to stress.

As excess sugar is stored as glycogen in the liver and extra fat is stored under the skin, added *stress* gets stored in the muscles. Most of us never notice muscle tension until it becomes chronic or extreme. Headaches, backaches and tightness in the neck and shoulders are signals that our mind is trying to communicate with us. If we learn to become aware of these internal mental cues before they escalate into torn ligaments, slipped disks and inflamed joints, we can prevent problems before they have a chance to develop. When we remain inattentive to all of our feelings and movements, it is easy to lose control over them.

For both professional and amateur athletes, however, the focus is still at the physical level. We are beginning to realize that performance is both a physical and mental endeavor, and that the mind plays a key role in whatever exercise we are involved in.

While competitive sports are good for us physically, they tend to drain us emotionally in one way or another. In such sports, the high intensity level leads to mental tension and depletion of energy. And though it is true that most exercise relieves stress, our muscles can *accumulate* it when we play contact sports or lift weights. If our focus is only on the next repetition or winning the game, we defeat the ultimate purpose of exercise: the release of muscle tension. Instead, like the muscles that tighten, the *mind* itself contracts.

176

Bryan is convinced that it was his state of mind during a NFL draft game that caused his knee to give out. He had been so nervous about playing in front of the scouts that he neglected to warm up or wear a brace on the knee that had already been bothering him. An additional stress was the emotional attachment he felt for the game—at that time, he could see no other future, or means of support for himself.

In this way, our *awareness* is focused externally when we have an intense desire to win or please the crowd. Thus, when our minds become *disengaged* from what our bodies are doing, we are more vulnerable to injury or a sense of loss.

Another negative component of competitiveness is racing against the clock, as in a marathon or swimming meet. Such behavior reinforces *time urgency* and *hostility*. Trying to fit in an entire workout in one half-hour, Mike would make business calls from his cellular phone while he was on the treadmill. His mind was so preoccupied with office work that when he attempted to bench-press excessive weight, he subsequently injured his lower back. A sense of *time-urgency* coupled with distraction had only caused him pain and injury. His workout did not alleviate his stress or provide him much physical conditioning. As Mike learned to regret, physical activity without full mental concentration does not yield us much benefit.

Modern physical therapy programs are beginning to rediscover the ancient yoga disciplines of concentration and mental imagery. Patients undergoing physical rehabilitation are first asked to create an image in their minds, to think about the physical goal they are working towards. They then successfully "perform" the action in their minds before they ever perform it physically. This kind of "guided imagery" can help alleviate chronic pain, fatigue and depression, among other ailments.

Yoga is the origin of *all* the martial arts, and for thousands of years, these martial artists have utilized the technique of intense concentration to increase their skill and mastery. Be it aerobics or martial arts, once the mind focuses completely, we become more skillful.

Seated as a restrained passenger, I was once severely injured in an automobile accident, sustaining multiple fractures. As a result, I walked with a limp gait, and gained about 25 pounds from inactivity. Several years of traditional physical therapy failed to overcome my handicap. Only after I came in contact with a Himalayan yogi and learned to apply his teachings, did I begin to truly heal from within.

The master not only taught me to incorporate several specific *hatha* yoga exercises for my back, but also instilled in me a sense of mindfulness. After incorporating the *asanas* with *pranayama,* I was able to regain my balance, and lost weight by walking 2 miles a day—without the limp.

The discipline of *hatha* yoga is described in the very translation of the word, basically meaning "to force." This force is far removed from the violent or painful force that a wrestler, boxer or weight lifter employs. Rather, *hatha* yoga implies that we are forcing our-selves to *overcome* a habit or tendency, like time-urgency, hostility, competitiveness, gluttony, abuse or laziness. Such a practice invokes an atmosphere in which positive change can occur.

If our body is rigid and inflexible—from either trauma or general inactivity—chances are that the same conditions are occurring somewhere in the mind. Making the body more flexible and adaptable, we allow the mind to become so as well.

Yoga is a gentle forcing that enhances the subtle energy field, and not just the physical body itself. No longer are we simply working from without, but are becoming engaged from within. From the superficial body consciousness, we start to encroach upon the deeper levels of inner *awareness.* By mending the mind, we become mindful of the body.

178

We usually relegate exercise to a specific time slot, experiencing an euphoric, but short-lived after-effect. The mindfulness cultivated in yoga, however, soon starts to spill over into our entire existence. Perhaps for the first time, we become aware of our carriage, posture and conduct. *Hatha* yoga is beyond exercise; it is much more than a *supplement* to other exercise, as it adds new dimension to life. Incorporating the practice encourages concentration, skillfulness and balance, and enhances performance.

Adhering to the natural rhythms, it is best to practice yoga early in the morning and again, after the sun sets, to gain maximum benefits. The cycle begins with the active, masculine power of the sunrise at dawn (corresponding with right nostril breath in *pranayama*) and ends with the intuitive, feminine emergence of the moon at dusk (corresponding with left nostril breath). Evoking both the force of the sun and the moon (*ha* meaning sun, and *tha* meaning moon), *hatha* then becomes the key to understanding how each of us shares a personal relationship with the cyclical universe.

When we make our appointment to practice our yoga routine, our entire being is engaged, as the emphasis is on the energy. Once there is total synchrony between body and mind, there is effective distribution of *prana* throughout the system. What results is peace of mind, proportion of body... and a balance of both. At once energized and relaxed, we feel a sense of fulfillment.

Hatha yoga utilizes the breath as the vital link between the body and mind, so coordinating the breath with every movement is essential. Although both yoga and *calisthenics* involve stretching, breath control dramatically improves our capacity to stretch. The slow, sustained movements in yoga loosen tight muscles in a way that rapid, jerking ones more common to regular calisthenics can not simulate.

A general rule is to synchronize the mind with each movement: inhaling first, exhaling next as we stretch or bend, and inhaling once again, as we return to the original position. With each exhalation, we gradually extend our capacity to stretch.

Yoga strengthens our spine and prepares our body to sit in meditation, as most of the postures are centered around the nervous system. The balanced movements and postures help coordinate the left-brain and right-brain hemispheres, enhancing creativity and sharpening the intellect.

Yoga is fluid movement, like a dance, and we develop the flexible limbs and graceful carriage of a dancer. Aesthetically, a yogi is as pleasing to the eye as beautiful artwork. Emotionally, he or she will gain clarity, stability, and become capable of weathering difficult situations.

Perfect control of the mind should precede the actions of the body. In yoga, we rediscover how to use inner *awareness* as a motivational tool to do just that. As yoga purifies the body internally, it removes the grime and impurities collected daily: misdirected passion or lust, excessive anger or pride, greed, sorrow and despair. When the mind is unblemished, we find our ability to concentrate much improved. With concentration comes a mastery of the senses, and this control is what enables us to attain *saucha,* or purity.

Perhaps that is why yogis and long-time yoga practitioners retain their youthfulness even very late in life. Their acquired contentment and tranquility defer the aging process as much as the *asanas* keep their bodies supple and flexible. Exercise is one factor that has been shown to retard the effects of aging. Things that able and healthy people take for granted—walking up a flight of stairs, or moving about unaided—are often impossible feats for those who have become frail and stiff from age and related inactivity.

Elderly individuals who make fitness part of their lives continue to function as before, and are more likely to out-live sedentary seniors. A study conducted at Tufts University on nursing home residents—the eldest being 96, the youngest 87—cited that muscle tone and strength increased more than 100% with rehabilitative weight training. The subjects reported improved coordination, balance and activity as well. Within eight weeks, residents in the study also regained their ability to walk and move about freely.

The great yogi Iyengar, who does not believe that old age should ever equal inactivity, says: "Just as an unbaked earthen pot dissolves in water the body soon decays. So bake it hard in the fire of yoga discipline in order to strengthen and purify it."

By practicing yoga, our small worlds become larger "arenas," encompassing infinite *awareness*. Like the once-infirm Iyengar, we can also overcome our physical handicaps and self-doubt once we take control of the "reins," and conduct the "horses." As the newly confident driver of the "chariot," we are able to focus our *awareness* and reclaim our freedom of mind, body and soul.

Chapter Nineteen

Appointment with Self

Yoga is not just a physical exercise...
it is finding yourself within yourself
by removing worldly thoughts from the mind.
—master yogi Baba Hari Dass

The very essence of yoga means "union," connecting not only the body to the mind and the mind to the soul, but yoking the single individual to the entire cosmos. The term *hatha* yoga describes the *asanas,* the physical aspect of the practice. *Pranayama* links the breath—the physical aspect of the mind—with the movement, just as meditation brings the lower self and the higher Self together. In this way, yoga promotes physical, mental and emotional tranquility as it conditions and tones the body, and calms and purifies the mind...so that the path to spirit is made clear.

People in general, my patients included, have a misconception that yoga is only for the "human pretzel," who contorts the body into impossible postures, and emphasizes only the physical aspect of the practice. This is "Hollywood yoga," because it is more of a total body workout than anything. Scientists and psychologists employ biofeedback methods for mind control to simulate yoga in labs and experiments, but the only kind that results is "Harvard yoga." The only yoga, however, that incorporates mind, body and soul is "Himalayan yoga": *hatha* yoga for the body, *pranayama* for the mind and *meditation* for the soul.

Mend the Mind

Hatha not only implies a gentle "forcing"of the physical body, but a"forcing out" of negative habits, tendencies, and unchecked desires as well. Before we can ever truly be free of any hindrance, we must first overcome our fears, especially of the "other," and of death. Preoccupation with fear is a constant drain on our energy resources and dampens our creativity, so much so that our *awareness* becomes obstructed and contracted.

Once we conquer fear, we can tame our seemingly "uncontrollable" urges, and channel our energy constructively. By developing the power of discrimination, we can begin to make more intelligent choices and cultivate a sense of mental dispassion. Our *awareness* then expands, and unfolds our power within to replace our negative mindset with love, joy, tranquility and will.

We gain access to our "inner world" through *pranayama*, and there are many variations to the practice. The deep, even diaphragmatic breath itself is the foundation for them all. The breathing exercises mend, or train the mind to develop internal energy dynamics needed in other yoga practices.

The focus of basic alternate nostril breathing is an equal number of inhalations and exhalations through the right and left nostrils. This balanced alternation has a calming and synchronizing effect on our mind. Such simple breath awareness is an ideal preparation for deep relaxation and meditation. When interspersed with the *asanas*, or other aerobic exercise, it also increases our inner balance and coordination.

If possible, *pranayama* should be practiced three times a day: early morning, late afternoon and later in the evening. In about five to ten minutes, sixteen rounds should complete one full cycle. Ideally, each set is repeated three times. Between each cycle, it is beneficial to take three deep, even diaphragmatic breaths through both nostrils simultaneously.

Advanced *pranayama* is often accompanied by breath retention, but it requires constant guidance from a competent instructor. Just as wild animals are tamed gradually, so *prana* must be carefully controlled, step-by-step, through consistent and diligent practice.

Learning to "rebreathe" naturally, we dispel mental stress and related illnesses, creating a tranquil environment within. We learn to appreciate solitude, and no longer suffer loneliness. Fortified by our inner strength, we understand that it is not the world that is confused...it is that we live in a confused mind.

Mind the Body

We begin our daily practice by lying in *shavasana*, or "corpse pose," to help eradicate any existing tension in the mind and body. Here we lie in a state of "ultimate relaxation," with our arms lying away from the torso, palms open. Our spine is pressed flat into the floor so we feel that the lower back is being supported. As of yet, there is no pressure or demand on any part of the body, and we relax by taking deep diaphragmatic breaths to prepare for practice.

"Corpse" posture is also utilized as a break, or pause in between *asanas* as a way to recharge and conserve our resources. In such deep relaxation, we visualize the body as a hollow vessel and focus the mind on the breath. With the inhalation, we imagine that a wave of soft blue light containing "vital energy" is slowly filling and illuminating us. With each exhalation, we empty ourselves of this light, as if all the unwanted thoughts and mental blemishes are being washed away with it.

We engage in breath *awareness* while we lie like a "corpse," becoming fully relaxed in about five minutes.

After relaxation, yoga practice commences with the *sun salutation*.

184

The sun is virtually the prime source of energy, which directly or indirectly furnishes all life on earth. Ancient cultures have always worshipped the sun, among them many Native American tribes, and the Aztec civilizations in Mexico. These indigenous cultures devised ceremonies celebrating the bright star, usually in the form of a sun dance.

Performing the *sun salutation* "bakes" our body in the yoga fire of discipline, strength and purity, and generates *tapas*, or heat. Igniting our effort to achieve a goal, and providing us with stamina until we reach it, *tapas* acts as our own small, inner sun.

To eventually flow through the *asanas* with momentum, precision and grace is our goal, and with the creation of physical warmth in the body, we are more likely to achieve it.

An integrated exercise that improves both physical coordination and mental reflexes, the *sun salutation* "salutes" the rising of the sun and the dawn of a new day.

Upon awakening, we make a remarkable transition from inertia to activity. In sleep, our metabolic rate decreases, circulation and heart beat slow down, and bodily functions quieten.

Awakening the body by creating *tapas*, the exercise gets circulation flowing and warms up the spine, joints and muscles so they become limber and supple. The *sun salutation* stimulates and massages the glands, organs, muscles and nerves. Such calisthenic exercise clears away the cobwebs from sleep so that we become energized.

Since the entire sequence is coordinated with the breath, a *sun salutation* becomes a kind of rhythmic dance, a series of twelve positions (Fig.16) that flow together in one graceful, continuous movement. One *sun salutation* completes a cycle, and for a beginner, performing three to five cycles is a wonderful transition from sleep to wakefulness.

FIGURE 16. SUN SALUTATION

Sun Salutation

1. Salutation: Begin standing tall with a straight spine, and feet together on the mat. Weight is distributed evenly on both feet, and hands are placed —palms together— in front of the chest, as in *Namaste*, or "prayer." Exhale, and concentrate on the breath.

2. Raised Arm: On the inhalation, extend the arms over the head, lifting and expanding the chest and arching the spine backwards. Allow the head to look upward, and keep breathing evenly.

3. Hand to Foot: On the exhalation, bend the torso forward and down, as far as it is comfortable. Do not lock the knees, let them soften or bend freely. Keeping the shoulders and elbows relaxed, bring the hands to the floor.

4. Equestrian: Inhaling, extend the left leg back, and rest the left knee on the mat. The front right knee is bent, and the supporting foot remains flat on the floor. Palms resting on either side of the right foot, lift the spine and open the chest.

5. Push-Up: Exhaling, step the right leg back so both legs are straight. With the support from the arms, keep the spine neutral, inhaling again.

6. Crocodile: Lower the knees, slide the chest and then the chin to the mat on the exhalation. Keep elbows close to the sides of the body, and continue to move into the next pose.

7. Cobra: On the inhalation, lift and expand the chest forward and up, supporting the weight of the upper body with the palms of the hands. Keep the pelvis flat on the floor, and the head reclined, continuing to breathe.

8. Mountain: With an exhale, raise the buttocks and hips, shifting the weight back on the heels. Lengthen through the back of the

legs by pressing heels into the floor, and the heels of the palms away from the body.

9. Equestrian: Inhale, step the right leg forward between the hands. The left leg stays extended back, knee to the ground. The front knee should be bent, with the foot flat on the floor. Extend the spine and head, and lift the chest forward and up.

10. Hand to Foot: Exhaling, step the left leg forward to meet the right. As both hands remain on the floor, let the knees soften or bend freely into a forward bend.

11.Raised Arm: On the inhalation, lift the arms from the upper back, opening the chest forward and up. Continuing to lift and expand the chest, extend the arms over the head. Keep the breathing smooth and even.

12. Salutation: Exhale, lowering the arms, and return the hands to "prayer" position. This completes one cycle of the *sun salutation*. On the subsequent *salutations*, continue to alternate which foot is extended back, and which one steps forward, as in Equestrian positions 4 and 9.

There are 86 *asanas* in yoga, each one representing human evolution through 86,000 species. Such postures anthropomorphized by yogis include the tree, the locust, the crocodile, the dolphin, the swan, the dog, an embryo and an upright warrior. By positioning ourselves into living manifestations other than the average human form, we are taught to respect and revel all life as equal.

Before engaging in yoga, or an exercise program of any kind, getting medical clearance is best. For beginners like Nicole, Bryan, Mike, Joe, Andre and Erin, it is essential to have the supervision of a competent yoga instructor. To learn about *asanas* other than the *sun salutation*, I refer them to *Light on Yoga* by B.K.S. Iyenger, referred to as the "Bible" of *hatha* yoga practice.

By practicing the asanas, we not only maintain a supple, healthy body but physically prepare ourselves to sit in meditation for an extended period of time. Likewise, pranayama strengthens the mind, allowing for the ascension of *awareness*.

Meet the Soul

Sitting in a steady, correct posture—with a straight head, neck and spine— is the most essential ingredient in meditation. Only then can the energy finds its way from the root of the spine to the crown of the head.

Sitting comfortably, tall and centered, gently close the eyes and establish smooth, even diaphragmatic breathing through the nose. Find a regular rate and rhythm for the breath, so from breath *awareness*, the mind is cleared of all non-essential thoughts, and is finally able to withdraw from all spaces and places.

We can then survey or scan the entire body systematically –from the top of the head to the toes—to release any tension or discomfort that we observe along the way. Continuing to concentrate on the breath, we begin to utilize visualization technique, like focusing on a candle flame, or intoning a *mantra*. Furthermore, we create inner resonance by focusing on the specific *mantra*, and visualization of each *chakra*. This intonation and mental imagery guides us through the progression of *chakras* and unleashes the power of *kundalini* energy.

Such focus helps to keep our mind from wandering, and brings it back to a center if it does. Our goal is to allow thoughts, images, and memories flow by without reacting to them. Rather than become swayed by, or critique, the contents of the mind, we simply "witness" them.

The key to meditation is to practice it for as long as it is comfortable. For beginners, this may be about five to ten minutes. Only gradually should this time be extended, to twenty or thirty minutes. Our inner clock will usually guide us, letting us know when enough time has elapsed. When we finish, we slowly bring our hands up to cover our eyes and open them into our palms. Removing our palms from our eyes, we return again to the external world. Stepping off the mat, we carry with us our meditative reward of *breath* and *mantra awareness*, with which we can *maintain* a calm center within throughout the entire day...this is what is known as "meditation in action."

To illustrate this, there is a fable that describes a meeting between a royal king and a learned young man. Upon his return to the city, the young man's father, a minister in the king's court, introduced him to his Majesty. His Highness welcomed the young man to admire the damsels, jewels and opulence in his palace. As a test, the king challenged him to carry a bowl filled to the brim with oil throughout his tour of the palace...without dropping a single drop. If he dared to drop the oil, he would face dire consequences.

After the tour, the king asked the young man what he had seen. The young man's reply was, "Nothing." The king then explained to the young man that by focusing not on the surrounding riches, but on only his task at hand, he had unknowingly simulated the art of meditation. If, even while enjoying the royal riches, the young man could accomplish the same, he would be performing meditation in action!

Once mastered, the practice of meditation enhances our perspective of life and becomes a vehicle for personal growth and transformation. The inner experience opens our everyday vistas to wider horizons, expanding our *awareness*.

In deep meditation, a sensation of light floods our entire being, as the mind and body are transcended ...to meet the soul.

Chapter Twenty

Infinite Awareness

When one sees eternity in things that pass away
and infinity in finite things, then one has pure knowledge.
But if one merely sees the diversity of things, with their
divisions and limitations, then one has impure knowledge.
And if one selfishly sees a thing as if it were everything,
independent of the one and the many,
then one is in the darkness of ignorance.
—from the Bhagavad Gita

The beauty of yoga philosophy lies in its Universal Reality: from the infinitesimally small organism at the bottom of the ocean to the eternal stretch of the sky high above, all life is interconnected.

The entire universe is a dynamic pattern of energy interference, with an "implicate" order. What Nicole, Bryan and most of us had never realized before was this inherent truth: that every piece contains the whole and every single aspect of the universe represents the entire cosmic picture. We are microcosms within the universal macrocosm; just as we mirror the universe, the universe is reflected within us.

The interconnectedness of nature weaves an intricately woven web at the sub-atomic level. The "solidity" of matter dissolves, and simply becomes an illusion to the senses. We then experience the universe as a dynamic, inseparable whole, which always includes us as the "observer." Becoming both the actor *and* the spectator in the unfolding drama of existence, the distinction between "I" (microcosm) and "the world" (macrocosm) disappears.

The holographic interconnectedness defines all-inclusive reality, which is omniscient, omnipresent and omnipotent. This Universal Reality is existence itself—free, self-aware and inherently blissful. In yoga philosophy, it is referred to as *Sat-Chit-Ananda*, or *Existence-Consciousness-Bliss*...literally capturing the essence of body-mind-soul!

True Reality has no beginning and no end. This *potential* energy is free and independent from concepts like time, space or causation. From the freedom of a *non-dual* existence comes the natural expression of peace.

This Undifferentiated Reality within the microcosm is called *Purusha*—the pure Self, or soul that is "ever free, ever pure and ever wise." Our individual ever-flowing *awareness* is a reflection of *Purusha*, or pure consciousness. Distinct from thoughts—we know *what* we are thinking and we know *that* we are thinking—*awareness* is greater than the contents of the mind. It is a fundamental ground for all experience, and can not be expressed in any language, for it is non-verbal.

To symbolize *awareness*, Apollo XIV astronaut Edgar D. Mitchell, in his book *Psychic Exploration*, adapted the Greek letter *Omega*. It coincides with the universal mantra *Om*—the cosmic vibration central to yoga. Interestingly, his experience in outer space converges with our investigation of "inner space."

Through this voyage, we encounter worlds of existence beyond the barriers of the here and now, spiritual galaxies far above the artificial and material world. The spiritual universe is *infinite* and unobstructed—beyond ordinary senses and perceptions—but our material world is *finite* and rather limited.

Yoga wisdom leaves a lasting impression on us. From our daily meditations, we become intoxicated, imbibed with the vibrations of pure *awareness*. As we explore the frontiers of our own *awareness*, the answers to our initial questions emerge. *Awareness* thus becomes the meeting ground of Reality—both *within* and *without*.

Perhaps what makes certain individuals outstanding is their unobstructed *awareness*. Gandhi fasted for an inordinate amount of time, yet he remained at peace. Beethoven produced many brilliant compositions, despite his deafness.

Such individuals do not necessarily think more, or harder, than the rest of the world; they are simply *aware*. From the invisible domains beyond the senses, *awareness* is expressed in many forms, including humanitarianism, art, science, invention and philosophy.

Mike overcame his *time-urgency* and *hostility*; both Joe and Erin regained their health and zest for life; Nicole achieved *tranquility* without tranquilizers. What made them *aware*, and enabled them to redirect their energies in a more positive way was yoga and meditation. Although they had all first turned to contemporary medicine, their true inner healing began only when they made their "appointment with Self."

The same *awareness*, when misdirected, causes us to desire and indulge in excessive sensual pleasures, thrill seeking and even violence. A meditative lifestyle does not necessarily make us desireless, but diminishes our non-essential attachments to situations, objects and people. It is not the *desire*—want of repeat pleasure or avoidance of pain—that so often leads us astray. It is our uncontrolled urges and our *dependency* on fulfilling these desires that cause us distress.

By becoming mindful, we begin to make the right choices, and overcome dependency by cultivating the powers of discrimination.

Through physical and mental *deconditioning*, we are then able to refrain from acting on impulse.

Mike had once dealt with his anger by indulging in alcohol; Joe reacted to environmental stress by smoking; Erin remained sleepless and pessimistic about the future; Nicole relied on Valium to curb her anxiety; Bryan developed high cholesterol from poor eating habits, generally taking his health for granted. Through yoga and meditation, all of them reclaimed their lost health by fortifying their "inner worlds." Their newly discovered powers of discrimination and *mindfulness* allowed them to make better choices. Even though they are faced with the same external situations, they have learned to *act, not react*.

Andre admitted that turning to drugs was a way to instantly "escape" his problems and boost his low self-worth. What he achieved was only a transient, "artificial high" with dire consequences, for material things never fully supplement what is lacking in our "inner world." They only serve to cause further dependency.

When we meditate, we possess quiet power, and free ourselves from non-essential thoughts. Providing an everlasting "natural high," meditation opens wider vistas of infinite *awareness* rather than narrow "escape" routes.

Meditation not only grants us *tranquility*, but also encourages our inner talents to shine. It is no coincidence that Andre was able to eventually kick his drug habit once he began to meditate. His creativity, which had remained dormant for some time, found its expression in poetry once again.

Daily practice will reveal our higher powers within, loosening the chains of dependency, fear and self-condemnation that bind us. The meditative mind not only helps us tame our urges, but also makes us more accepting of who we are so that we can transform "issues" into "non-issues."

Meditation transports us to a timeless, boundless *awareness* where we can dwell in a blissful state, becoming one with the soul. The body seeks pleasure, the mind, happiness and the heart, joy. But only in the fourth dimension of spiritual *awareness* are we eternally blissful. Unlike pleasure to pain, happiness to unhappiness and joy to sorrow, there is no *antonym* for bliss.

Even though *awareness* is indestructible, our *aliveness* is inevitably subject to entropy or death. Our physical body exists as a temporal or earth-bound reality, and is under the influence of time, space, gravity and causation.

Before it manifests in the physical body, illness is a distortion in the subtle energy field. Be it acquired or "carried over" from previous lifetimes, this warp determines illness, as balance denotes wellness. Once we understand that our "hidden physiology" is an energy field—that *we are energy* and that *we need energy*—we can begin to comprehend why some people seem immune to disease or disorder, and why others are routinely at risk.

Health truly is a mind-body-soul discipline. We have the ability to enhance our mental, physical and spiritual well being. From within, we develop physical and emotional immunity, which prevents disease and reduces the intensity of an existing illness.

How true were the yoga masters when they affirmed: *"All human suffering is ignorance. Awareness is freedom."* Once we apply this fundamental truth, the secrets of health and longevity are revealed!

Enhancing our *chit*, or *awareness*, and controlling the *prana*, or *aliveness*, opens the door to understanding. How long and how well we will live in our physical body is determined by our own actions, choices and behaviors. If we remain unaware, and take our health for granted, how can we expect to live long and healthy lives?

To achieve spiritual *awareness*, a stable mind and body is essential. "Taking it easy" when it comes to health eventually results in "dis-ease." Health can not be purchased in a doctor's office or a pharmacy—it is a lifetime commitment.

Traditional medicine mostly fails to address the "unseen" realm of energy. It also neglects to recognize our ability to access and influence the vital force. Our dependency on the instant relief that is provided by medication often encourages personal neglect and "mindlessness." If we rely only on external means and "quick fixes," we remain unaware of the healing power within. Naturally, I honor modern medicine and its command of emergency situations, surgical interventions and comfort measures, but most of it *is* "after the fact."

Holistic methods acknowledge the "unseen connection" of mind, body and soul, and are thus able to evade illness and restore wellness. This "uncommon wisdom" is no longer a secret or something out of reach. The yoga discipline and meditative lifestyle provides inner balance, working to prevent health problems "before the fact."

Although validated by science, yoga is *experiential* in nature. Once given the opportunity to explore, we must experience it to prove it to ourselves. The greatest impediments to our own practice are procrastination and self-doubt. Now is the time to resolve, to become architects of our own destiny and take control. It is read in the *Puranas*, the ancient scriptures:

> *While this body is yet free of disease and*
> *the old age is yet far away*
> *while the strength in the senses yet waxes and*
> *the lifespan is not in ebb,*
> *the wise man must right now undertake*
> *endeavors for spiritual uplifting*
> *for, what effort to dig a well*
> *when the house is already on fire.*

First and foremost, we compromise our health and longevity when we are *out of phase* with the cosmic rhythms. Mindfulness of our own bodily rhythms is an essential discipline. When we regulate our meals, activities and sleep times, our body clock remains in harmony with the natural order of things. For instance, making morning meditation the *first appointment* of the day helps put us on track.

Consistent practice of dietary *awareness* and yoga adds years to our own lifespan. The essence of our mind emanates from what we ingest, and the "gastric fire" is kept well regulated by exercise. Likewise, becoming a "professional sleeper" conserves our resources by dispensing away with energy-consuming dream states. Quality sleep equals quality meditation.

Through *pranayama*, we can regain control of our *aliveness* and defer *entropy*. As the main instrument for breath control, our nose is the strategic link between the physical body and the "inner world." By becoming more "breath friendly," we overcome emotional over-load and achieve tranquility.

Taking slow and deep breaths increases our breathing efficiency. By economizing *prana*, we are literally able to "cheat our Creator"! The diaphragm, after all, is the very last muscle to fatigue at the time of death. When we breathe our last breath, it is said that we "expire." This literally describes the function of the much-ignored diaphragm, or "spiritual muscle." The *Munduaka Upanishad* teaches that:

> *In whom the heaven, earth, and sky*
> *Are interwoven as well as the mind with all the pranas-*
> *Know that One alone as Self.*
> *Abandon all other speeches,*
> *This alone is the bridge of immortality.*

Transiting from life cycle to life cycle, *awareness* renders us immortal. Death may be a termination of *aliveness*, but is merely a transition for *awareness*. At the time of excarnation, or death, the entire field of *awareness* converges to a quintessential point. Encapsulating the pure Self or soul, it transmigrates *faster* than the speed of light...only to find another beginning.

This "migratory bird"—which is comprised of the subtle and causal body and the soul— leaves behind the physical body. The *matter* is returned to the elements, and the *prana* is released once again to the free energy of the universe. The entire *samskaras*, or lifetime experience contained therein, are thus "carried over" from one life cycle to another.

The cycle of *samsara*, or transmigration, is depicted very powerfully in one of the *Yoga Upanishads*. The passage symbolizes the cosmic wheel in motion, comprised of the uninterrupted chain of deaths and rebirths:

> *It is happy, the child that sucks*
> *at its mother's breast;*
> *it is the same breast it*
> *fed from in a former life!*
> *The husband takes his pleasure*
> *in his wife's belly*
> *he was conceived in the past!*
> *He who was the father*
> *is today the son.*
> *and that son, when tomorrow comes,*
> *will be a father in his turn;*
> *thus, in the flow of samsara*
> *men are like the buckets*
> *around a water wheel!*

In the cosmic cycle, birth and death are passages or transitions, and life occupies the interval between birth and death. Birth, *not* life, is the true opposite of death, for life is a continuum. Life is ever evolving, and its purpose is a thirst for higher *awareness* which

198

can only be quenched... by mending the mind, minding the body and meeting the soul.

From womb to tomb, our life follows like the chapters in a book. Death is not the end of the story, but an epilogue instead. It is not a terminal event, but a predecessor to rebirth—the gateway to a new beginning. Each rebirth is yet another prologue in the book of life, introducing the next edition. Did not Benjamin Franklin prepare one of the most famous of American epitaphs?

"The body of Benjamin Franklin, printer, like the cover of an old book, its contents torn out and striped of its lettering and gilding, lies here, food for worms, but the work shall not be lost. For it will appear once more in a new and more elegant edition, revived and corrected by the author."

Glossary

Ahankara: Ego

Ahimsa: Non-violence; Abstaining from causing injury to a living being.

Asana: Posture(s) that are performed during the practice of Yoga.

Ayurveda: Ancient Indian medical science.

Bhagavad Gita: The "Song of the Lord;" part of the ancient Mahabharata epic in which Lord Krishna teaches Yoga to his disciple Arjuna, on the battlefield of Kurukshetra approximately 5000 years ago.

Brahmamuhurta: "Hour of the Lord;" auspicious hour.

Brahman: Universal Reality.

Buddhi: Intellect.

Chakra: Center of Consciousness.

Chit: Awareness; Consciousness.

Chitta: Individual Consciousness.

Dharna: Concentration; fixation of the mind on one point.

Dhyana: Meditation.

Hatha Yoga: Physical discipline of Yoga.

Ida: Left main subtle energy channel.

Karana Sharira: Causal body.

Karma: Law of cause and effect operating on the metaphysical level, such that each and every action produces (in time and space) an equal and opposite reaction.

Kundalini: Coiled up dormant potential energy which lies at the base of the spine.

Mudra: Pose.

Om (AUM): Mantra representing the Universal Reality.

Parimanu: Atom.

Pingala: Right main subtle energy channel.

Prana: Aliveness; Vital life force; subtle life energy.

Pranayama: Breath control.

Purusha: Soul; Self; Spirit.

Samadhi: Enstasy; Higher consciousness attained through Yoga.

Samsara: Transmigration; cycles of birth and death.

Samskara: Subconscious subtle impressions that are created whenever an action is performed. Remain latent until triggered by circumstance to release impulses.

Sat-Chit-Ananda: Existence-Consciousness-Bliss; the aspects of Universal Reality.

Shakti: Power, Divine Energy.

Sthula Sharira: Physical Body.

Sukshma Sharira: Subtle Body.

Sushumna: Centrally located subtle energy channel.

Turiya: The fourth state, beyond the states of waking, dream and dreamless sleep.

Upanishads: Series of nearly 200 texts composed between 800 and 500 BC.

Vedas: Series of four books containing mystical hymns and mantras. Composed in the fifth millenium BC, assumed written form by 1200 BC.

Yoga: the yoking of all the powers of body, mind and spirit.

Yoga Nidra: Conscious sleep.

Yoga Sutras: Text written by sage Patanjali codifying the science of Yoga.

References

A. Einstein, *"The Principle of Relativity"* (New York: Dover, 1923)

D. Bohm and B. Hiley, *"On the Intuitive Understanding of Nonlocality as Implied by Quantum Theory,"* Foundations of Physics, Vol.5, 1975, pp.93-109

I. Prigogine and I. Stengers, *"Order Out Of Chaos: Man's New Dialogue With Nature"* (New York: Bantam Books, 1984)

J. Briggs and F. Peat, *"David Bohm's Looking-Glass Map,"* in *Looking Glass Universe: The Emerging Science of Wholeness* (New York: Simon & Schuster, Inc.,1984)

G. Hodson, *"The Miracle of Birth: A Clairvoyant Study of a Human Embryo"* (1929;reprint, Wheaton, IL: Theosophical Publishing House, 1981)

H.S. Burr, *"The Fields of Life"* (New York: Ballantine Books, 1972)

S. Kirlian & V. Kirlian, *"Photography Visual Observations by Means of High Frequency Currents,"* Journal of Scientific and Applied Photography, vol.6 (1961)

I.Dumetrescu and J.Kenyon, *"Electrographic Imaging in Medicine and Biology"* (Suffolk, Great Britain: Neville Spearman Ltd., 1983)

W. Tiller, *"The Positive and Negative Space/Time Frames as Conjugate Systems,"*in *Future Science*, ed. White and Krippner (Garden City, NY: Doubleday & Co., Inc., 1977)

Appendix

W. Tiller, " *Some Energy Field Observations of Man and Nature*," in *The Kirilian Aura*, ed. Krippner and Rubin (Garden City, NY: Anchor Press/Doubleday, 1974)

H. Motoyama, "*Theories of the Chakras: Bridge to Higher Consciousness*" (Wheaton, IL: Theosophical Publishing House, 1981)

"*Electronic Evidence of Auras, Chakras in UCLA Study,*" Brain/Mind Bulletin, vol.3, no.9 (March20, 1978).

I. Stevenson, "*Involuntary memories during severe physical illness or injury,*" in *Journal of Nervous & Mental Disease*.183 (7): 452-8,1995 Jul.

Swami Rama, "*The Awakening of Kundalini,*" in *Kundalini: Evolution and Enlightenment,* ed. J. White (St. Paul, Minnesota: Athena Books, 1990)

I. Bentov, "*Micromotion of the Body as a Factor in the Development of the Nervous System,*" in *Kundalini: Evolution and Enlightenment*, ed. J. White (St. Paul, Minnesota: Athena Books, 1990)

S. Hagelin, "*Restructuring physics from its foundation in light of Maharishi's Vedic Science,*" Modern Science and Vedic Science, 3,3-71(1989)

J. Goldman, "*Healing Sounds: The Power of Harmonics,*" Element (Rockport, MA, 1992)

R. Reiter and J. Robinson, "*Melatonin: Your body's natural wonder drug,*" (New York: Bantam Books, 1995)

W. Pierpaoli and C. Yi, "*The involvement of the pineal gland and melatonin in immunity and aging,*" Journal of Neuroimmunology, 27,99-109

J. Ayres, et al. "*Chemical and Biological Hazards in Food,*" (New York: Hafner Publ, 1969)

I. Swann, "*To Kiss Earth Good-Bye*" (New York: Dell Publishing Co., Inc., 1975)

Recommended Reading

Sartre, Jean-Paul. *Nausea*. New Directions Publishing Co., 1964.

Capra, Fritjof. *The Tao of Physics*. New York: Bantam Books, 1988

Hesse, Herman. *Siddhartha*. New York: New Directions, 1951

Talbot, Michael. *The Holographic Universe*. New York: HarperPerennial, 1992

Nietzsche, Friedrich. *Human, All Too Human—A Book for Free Spirits*. University of Nebraska Press, 1984.

McCoy, Edain. *The Sabbats—A New Approach to Living the Old Ways*. Edain McCoy, 1994.

Vegetarian Times. *Vegetarian Times Complete Cookbook*. MacMillan, 1995.

Martins, Peter. *New York City Ballet Workout*. Peter Martins and New York City Ballet Company. William Morrow and Co. 1997.

Varenne, Jean. *Yoga and the Hindu Tradition*. Chicago: The University of Chicago Press, 1976.

Mascaro, Juan. *The Upanishads*. Great Britain: Penguin Books, 1988

Hoff, Benjamin. *The Tao of Pooh*. New York: Penguin Books, 1982.

Frawley, David. *Beyond the Mind*. Salt Lake City, Utah: Passage Press, 1992.

Waterhouse, J.M., Minors, D.S. & Waterhouse, M.E. *Your Body Clock*. Great Britain: Oxford University Press, 1990

Gerber, Richard. *Vibrational Medicine*. New Mexico: Bear & Company, 1988

Arya, Usharbudh. *Meditation And The Art Of Dying*. Pennsylvania: The Himalayan International Institute of Yoga Science and Philosophy, 1985

Nuernberger, Phil. *The Quest For Personal Power*. New York: G.P.Putnam's Sons, 1996

Swami Rajarshi Muni. *Awakening Life Force*. Minnesota: Llewellyn Publications, 1993

Iyengar, B.K.S. *Light On Yoga*. New York: Schocken Books.1977

Swami Rama, Ballentine, Rudolph & Hymes, Alan. *Science Of Breath*. Pennsylvania: The Himalayan International Institute of Yoga Science and Philosophy, 1990

Mehta, Gita. *A River Sutra*. New York: Nan A. Talese, Bantam Doubleday Dell Publishing Group, Inc., 1993

Weiss, Brian. *Many Lives, Many Masters*. New York: Fireside Book, Simon & Schuster Inc., 1988

Singh, Ranjie. *Self-Healing: Powerful Techniques*. London, Canada: A Health Psychology Associates Inc. Book.1997

Ballentine, Rudolph. *Diet & Nutrition: a holistic approach*. Pennsylvania: The Himalayan International Institute of Yoga Science and Philosophy, 1978

Morrison, Judith. *The Book of Ayurveda, A Holistic Approach to Health and Longevity*. London: Gaia Books Limited, 1995.

Ornish, Dean. *Program for Reversing Heart Disease*. New York: Ballantine Books, 1991.

Ornish, Dean. *Love & Survival*. New York: Harper Collins Publishers, Inc., 1998.

Index

About the Author

Raj Kapoor is a practicing internist who specializes in chest diseases and critical care medicine. He is a former chair of the Department of Medicine, UPMC Passavant, University of Pittsburgh Health System, Pennsylvania.

A recognized philosopher, Dr. Kapoor has lectured widely on lifestyle management, and he has been featured on numerous radio talk shows. He is an evocative writer who makes complex ideas thoroughly understandable with magical simplicity.

Raj Kapoor has explored the world of holistic thought through medicine and metaphysics, and sheds new light on the power of awareness in creating total freedom and perfect health.

Correspondence

Requests for information on workshops and seminars by
Dr. Kapoor or any personal correspondence can be
addressed to :

Center for Wellness

Suite 201, 9102 Babcock Blvd.
Pittsburgh, PA : 15237

(412)-FOR-WELL

Center for Wellness is unique in that it honors mental, physical and
spiritual well-being by taking into account the individual—genetics,
environmental factors, emotions, values and lifestyle habits—and offers
a personalized approach to healing the mind, body and soul.